CONTEMPORARY CHRISTIAN EDUCATION

The Ideal Christian Education Handbook

Micheal J. Darby

WESTBOW
PRESS®
A DIVISION OF THOMAS NELSON
& ZONDERVAN

WestBow Press books may be ordered through booksellers or by contacting:

WestBow Press
A Division of Thomas Nelson & Zondervan
1663 Liberty Drive
Bloomington, IN 47403
www.westbowpress.com
1 (866) 928-1240

Scripture taken from the King James Version of the Bible.

ISBN: 978-1-9736-2525-4 (sc)
ISBN: 978-1-9736-2524-7 (e)

Library of Congress Control Number: 2018904306

Print information available on the last page.

WestBow Press rev. date: 06/21/2018

Dedication

This book is dedicated to three of the finest Christian role models that I observed and communicated with during my Christian journey. They each lived over ninety years and were not college graduates but were spiritual graduates in honesty, love and compassion.

My grandfather James Walker Darby is the first that I will reference. He always had a word of wisdom. He would often say "It is no use worrying because it does not do any good" He was a loving, caring up right Christian role model. Several of his children preceded him in death and when he was notified he would say "the lord gives, and the lord takes away blessed is the name of the lord." He never wavered in his faith, he lived for Jesus throughout his life.

Mr. John Gardner a long-time Deacon and Sunday school superintendent of a church that I pastored is another person who demonstrated what it means to be a Christian. Deacon Gardner was, direct and honest. When he observed questionable or unchristian behavior he would request a private meeting to share his concerns. He was a man of strong Christian convictions and did not participate in negative gossip. He always looked for the positive in others rather than the negative. Deacon Gardner was an ultra-Christian role model for those in his presence.

The third person whom I dedicate this book to is Mrs. Lee Ella Brown Grissett a quiet, reserved lady who possessed the gift of love (the highest and most noble Christian quality); she was a member of the church where I presently attend; she possessed a loving smile and was just as beautiful on the inside as she was on the outside. Mrs. Grissett used the gift of love to bring joy in the lives of others, her kind words and loving behavior set an example for those around; her soft spirit of love will continue to live.

Every person writes a book during their journey through life and there is no control over who reads it. A person's words, behavior and deeds are constantly observed by others. It is essential to send positive Christian signals to those who live among us.

This book attempts to give an overview of most Church and Christian Education programs. Each chapter addresses a specific area of Christian Education. The resource materials in this book were accumulated over a thirty-year period. The author was inspired to write this book out of a love for Jesus Christ and the local church. It is hoped that those who read this book will be inspired to seek additional spiritual resources to increase their knowledge around Christian Education.

Author/Compiler Micheal J. Darby holds a BS degree in Psychology from Gardner Webb College, a Master of Divinity degree from Southeastern Theological Seminary in Wake Forest, North Carolina and a Master of Arts in Religious Education from Southwestern Theological Seminary in Fort Worth, Texas. The author is married and is the father of three adult children. He has served as a Pastor and as a Seminary Instructor of Christian Education and served as a State Convention denominational worker and he is a United States Army Veteran

Contents

The Role of the Pastor in Christian Education

The pastor is the chief overseer or shepherd of a church. The pastor can delegate responsibility, but ultimately, he is responsible for the success or failure of all church programs.

The Christian Education Ministry, the Program Committee, deacons, trustees, ushers, choir members and all officers of the Church have the obligation of informing the Pastor and acquiring his approval of all Church Programs.

A pastor has many roles, such as preacher, teacher, counselor, prophet, friend, role model, administrator and spiritual guide. All these roles are noble functions, which needs to be addressed if the pastor is to be effective in nurturing his flock to full Christian maturity.

Pastoring is the supreme Christian calling within a Church. The pastor must be submissive to the spirit of Jesus Christ for Jesus is the chief cornerstone of the church and when a pastor is totally obedient to the teachings of Christ, his flock is obligated to support him spiritually and financially to aid him in fulfilling the ministerial needs of the church.

The pastor who does not receive adequate spiritual and financial support from his flock is at a great disadvantage in fulfilling his basic pastoral needs. Christian Education is the responsibility of the entire church. The pastor and the flock have the responsibility of praying and working together as a team in building a sound Christian Education program.

The qualifications of a Bishop or Pastor are found in I Timothy 3:1-7 and in, Acts 20:28 and Titus 1:9

- **<u>Must be Blameless</u>** (I Timothy 3:2) one who has a good reputation and is a law abiding Christian citizen
- **<u>Husband of one wife</u>** (I Timothy 3:2) a faithful devoted husband who loves his wife and is committed to a monogamous marriage
- **<u>Vigilant, Sober and is of Good behavior</u>** (I Timothy 3:2) one who is focused and has a good reputation and is open to hospitality
- **<u>Not Given to Wine, no striker</u>** (I Timothy 3:3) one who is not given to wine or strong drink and is not a bully who belittles others
- **<u>Apt to Teach</u>** (I Timothy 3:2) one who can teach and is willing to receive instructions
- **<u>Not Greedy of Filthy Lucre</u>** (I Timothy 3:3) one who seeks first the Kingdom of God and His righteousness, and knows that material possessions bring no lasting satisfaction
- **<u>Able to maintain self-control</u>** (I Timothy 3:3) one who is not a brawler and is not covetous and knows how to control angry impulses and is not jealous of others
- **<u>Household management skills</u>** (I Timothy 3:4) one who knows how to manage his household by showing love and respect for his wife and children and can provide for their well-being
- **<u>Not a Novice</u>** (I Timothy 3:6) one who has experience in spiritual matters and has demonstrated Christian maturity in his speech and actions, and shows courage in the face of trials and tribulations
- **<u>Possess the Holy Ghost</u>** (Acts 20:28) one who is led by the Spirit of Jesus Christ and lives a Spirit filled life
- **<u>A Man of Honest Report</u>** (I Timothy 3:7) one who has a good reputation in the Church and within the community, a person who believes in wholesome Christian principles
- **<u>Knows the Word of God</u>** (Titus 1:9) one who understands the Teachings of the Scripture and is prepared to defend the Teachings of the Church

Christian Education Model

THE IMPORTANCE OF PRAYER

A church must pray for the leadership of the Holy Spirit in all Christian Education endeavors. Prayer is a very significant factor in the implementation of any religious program. Paul says in Philippians 4:6 "Be careful about nothing; but in everything by prayer and supplication with thanksgiving let your requests be known to God through prayer and supplication." (KJV) The serious steward of Christian Education is wise to follow Paul's advice of making their requests known to God through prayer and supplication.

Prayer makes a person aware of their own human frailties and limitations and at the same time leads a person to the realization that God's reservoir of strength and unlimited power can satisfy all human needs.

It is recommended that a church sponsor special quarterly or biannual Christian Education prayer sessions. This would highlight the significance of Christian Education and promote increased participation. As a distinctive feature, a qualified person could be invited to preach a sermon or give a short lecture on a specific area of Christian Education. It is also recommended that special prayer sessions be sponsored prior to major Christian Education workshops or seminar.

Jesus prayed to the Heavenly Father during the most challenging periods in his life. He was praying in the Garden of Gethsemane when Judas approached him with several soldiers who arrested him to stand trial before the Sanhedrin prior to his arraignment before Pontius Pilate. Jesus also prayed to the Father when he hung on the cross and said in Luke 23: 34Father, forgive them; for they know not what they do. Sincere prayer is the purest form of communication with the Heavenly Father.

CHRISTIAN EDUCATION MINISTRY

Together We Build

Establishing a Christian Education Ministry is essential to the success of a Christian Education program. Most Christian Education Ministries will include the:

- pastor as a standing member (ex officio)
- superintendent of the Sunday School
- several parents
- several teachers
- possibly a deacon or women's missionary leader
- youth representative

Many churches also include persons on the Christian Education Ministry who possess music, craft, organizational and teaching skills. Each church will need to select a method of structuring a Christian Education Ministry, which will satisfy its educational needs.

The following are two standard methods:

Method A: The pastor and nominating committee assigns a Director of Christian Education and authorizes the Director to select various individuals to serve on the Ministry with church approval.

Method B: The pastor and a special committee, with the church's approval, structure a Christian Education Ministry and then commission the Ministry to select a Director for the carrying on of business.

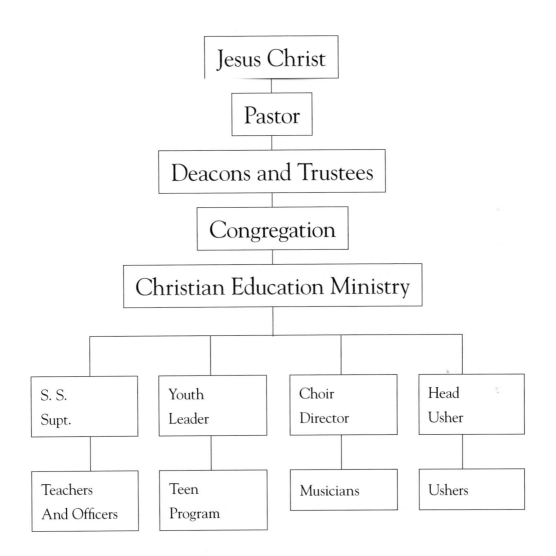

HOW TO PLAN AND COMMON STRATEGIES FOR PLANNING?

(Adopted from notes from a lecture given by Carlisle Driggers of the Southern Baptist Home Mission at the Ridgecrest Baptist Conference Center, August 1982)[1]

Planning is Important

How to Plan

- Planning should be practical, it should deal with what is possible
- Planning should be simple and open, there should be a clear understanding of plans
- Planning needs to be revised periodically to retain a degree of relevancy to overall goals and objectives
- Planning should be centered in prayer
- Planning should not be too detailed

General Categories of Plans

- 1 to 3 years short range planning
- 3 to 7 years medium range planning
- 7 to 25 years long range planning

WHY PLAN?

Planning increases effectiveness
Planning leads to positive results
Planning saves time Planning builds community
The Holy Spirit has a better opportunity to work

Calendar						
1	2	3	4	5	6	7
8	9	10	11	12	13	14
15	16	17	18	19	20	21
22	23	24	25	26	27	28

OUTLINE FOR PLANNING

- Identify your purpose
- Address your needs
- Discuss strategies to fulfill needs
- Pray for positive results
- Put plans into action

Planning for Training Worksheet

Session _____ Date _____ Topic _____

I want to achieve the following objectives:

a._____

b._____

c._____

What I want the trainees to know?

_____

_____

_____

_____

_____

(Adopted from notes from a lecture given by Carlisle Draggers of the Southern Baptist Home Mission at the Ridgecrest Baptist Conference Center Aug Conference Center, August 1 1982[2]

COMMON STRATEGIES FOR PLANNING

- Identify the purpose of the organization
- Study areas of need
- State specific objectives
- Establish goals (have statements of dates on measurable goals)
- Develop an action plan to set people in motion, assign someone to put a budget in place
- Evaluate plans semiannually, alter as needed

Early planning is essential to the success of all organizational programs. All individuals involved in Christian Education programming should value the importance of early planning and consistently work to see that good planning techniques are observed in all Christian Education endeavors.

IDENTIFYING EDUCATIONAL NEEDS

Each church can identify its educational needs and work toward satisfying those needs. Churches are like people, they have unique personalities. The cure or remedy in one church may be harmful in another church.

Knowing how to identify educational needs within the church is essential for spiritual growth and development. The Christian Education Ministry can serve as the prime organization for identifying educational needs.

Many churches have successfully identified educational needs by (1) random survey, (2) question answer sheet, or (3) personal conversations. However, maybe the most effective way of identifying the needs is to alert the Christian Education Ministry members and other responsible persons to report perceived needs to the Ministry on a regular basis.

Some Standard Christian Needs Are:

- prayer and quiet time
- bible study
- recreation
- tutoring
- current event discussion
- Christian growth discussions
- workshops and Christian Education Seminars

When standard Christian Education needs are met the spiritual life of the church is enhanced.

GOALS AND OBJECTIVES

When the Christian Education needs in a church are adequately listed and identified, the Christian Education Ministry should write clear, precise goals and objectives and state a specific plan to address those needs in compliance with the ministry of the church.

Many Christian Education Ministries are ineffective because they never follow through in achieving their desired goals and objectives. One of the best ways to monitor the progress of accomplishing goals and objectives is to schedule regular up-date reports.

These reports will eliminate a lot of guesswork, on which goals and objectives are being accomplished, and it would give the Christian Education Ministry members an opportunity to periodically modify strategies; which will increase desired program effectiveness. There are times when wrong goals and objectives are set for a given church. When this is apparent, the Christian Education Ministry has the responsibility of recognizing the problem and making the necessary corrections.

Lots of churches have lost valuable time by working on goals and objectives that were irrelevant to their Christian Education needs. Time is too important to be wasted on irrelevant goals and objectives. There is simply too much to be accomplished in the church and too many precious lives are affected.

Why have goals?

First goals help leaders to determine what is to be achieved in the teaching program. Second goals provide leaders with a sense of direction and a means of charting progress; finally, goals offer a target to achieve stated objectives.[3]

All writers of the Scripture had specific goals and objectives. The sheer volume of Paul's fourteen New Testament Books is evidence that Paul had a major influence on the first century Church. Paul was passionate in spreading the good news of Jesus Christ, his personal goals and objectives gave him a frame of reference to stay the course and maintain until his mission was accomplished.

PRACTICAL CHRISTIAN EDUCATION GOALS AND OBJECTIVES

Written Goals and Objectives are Important

The main goal of a Christian Education program is to provide training, leadership and guidance to the entire church community for ultimately leading them to full maturity in the Christian faith.

Goal Setting is Essential for Sound Church Programming

STANDARD OBJECTIVES

- sponsor workshops on Christian growth and development
- lead non-believers to a commitment to Jesus Christ as Lord and Savior
- encourage participation in missions, addressing human needs
- encourage participation in the full program of the church
- provide a strong Christian model
- expose all members to a variety of Christian ministries
- help members develop strong Bible study habits and to build effective prayer lives

All Church Workers Would Benefit from Reviewing Their Standard Objectives on a Regular Basis for Finding Ways to More Effectively Achieve Desired Program Results

Church Personnel Job Descriptions & Qualifications

CHURCH PERSONNEL JOB DESCRIPTIONS & QUALIFICATIONS

A Christian Education Ministry has the responsibility of developing its' own job descriptions. The spiritual and educational needs of the church determine the number of job descriptions. Before determining a job description, it is important to remember that a job description sets forth objectives, duties, relationships, and length of service and results expected of the person in the job.

Job descriptions should be written in a clear, precise language, which describes the specific duties of each church worker. Members need to know specifically what is required of them. A job description should spell out the duties of those who serve in specified church positions.

All Christians are Called to Labor in the Vineyard of Faith

Every believer is called to be a worker in the vineyard of Faith. The most successful Christian leaders knew what was expected of them. In many ways they had a job description. The Christian's job description is to teach what Jesus said when he was physically on Earth. We must let our lights shine so that others will see the love of Jesus in our words and actions. The behavior and the lifestyle of a believer has the greatest influence on the world around us.

SIX STEPS SUGGESTED IN WRITING JOB DESCRIPTIONS

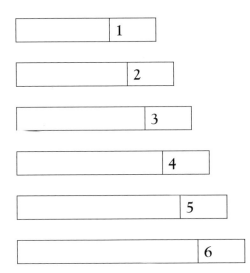

- Research materials from the State Convention and the church library to get some ideas of standard job descriptions of church workers
- Brainstorm to decide on what a Youth Director, Coordinator of Missions, etc. should be doing in your church.
- Discuss and decide on the most important and most relevant job description
- Assign a person to write the suggestions on a flip chart or chalk board
- Suggest revisions of the job descriptions, and then decide on the final revision
- Make sure the job descriptions are relevant to the needs of your church then put the final revisions of the job descriptions in print

It is very important that Christian leaders and believers write specific church job descriptions for church workers. Each church is unique what works in one church may not work in another. Every church has specific areas of ministry that need to be addressed. The best way to address these needs is to pray and brainstorm with other members and write the suggested solutions on paper and write and activate an action plan to address the needs.

STANDARD JOB DESCRIPTIONS OF CHURCH WORKERS

Let's Work Together

Pastor

- the spiritual shepherd or overseer of the congregation
- worship service leader
- preach the gospel message of Jesus Christ and lead members to the importance of Bible study
- lead the church in planning & setting goals and objectives
- conduct wedding ceremonies, funeral services, and special dedication services
- encourage members to pray for the guidance of the Holy Spirit
- approve the selection of staff positions
- serve as church moderator
- assist in the training of all staff members
- serves as a friend and counselor
- visit the sick and shut-in
- approve all church training and program activities
- appoint committees and councils
- lead the church in community service
- serve as an administrator
- conduct the Lord's Supper and conduct baptismal services
- serve as Christian role model
- promote the importance of family unity
- evaluate all church programs

The Sunday School Superintendent

- preside over the opening of Sunday School
- chief administrator of the Sunday School, presides over the collection of monies
- work with the Sunday School Secretary
- moderate procedures that require a vote
- work very closely with the pastor and the church

- recommend Sunday School teachers
- sponsor special Sunday School projects and events
- orders proper Sunday School materials
- monitor the amount of time spent in the individual's classes
- supervise the overall Sunday School program
- assign substitute teachers when a teacher is absent
- preside over the closing of the Sunday School session
- promote Sunday School growth and development, sponsor workshops and seminars

Sunday School Teacher

- teach the Sunday School Curriculum
- fellowship and work with the superintendent, the pastor, fellow teachers and members
- serves as a role model in the church and the community
- read and study lesson prior to teaching the class
- promote Sunday School growth
- share the good news of Jesus Christ
- maintain and keep good records
- contact absent students
- communicate with the superintendent to let him know about specific class needs

Secretary

- keeps a system of the program records
- records minutes of each board meeting
- reads minutes at each board meeting
- serves as the correspondent agent of the board

The Clerk

Qualifications

There are no special biblical qualifications for a secretary or clerk but there are certain general skills a secretary or clerk should possess to be an effective church officer such as:

Essential Clerk Qualities

- honesty and Christian Character
- legible hand writing
- good recall and memory
- a knowledge of bookkeeping
- the ability to relate with the public
- patience, promptness and dependability

The Duties of the Clerk

- keep accurate minutes at regular and special church meetings
- notify absent committee members, concerning specific minutes
- keep church rolls, maintain accurate names and addresses
- preserve past records, keep official records and documents in a secure location
- post announcements and church publicity
- prepare special reports on various church activities
- receives letters of transfer, sends out letters of dismissals

Treasurer

The position of treasurer is one of the most important positions in the church. Lots of challenging work and dedication goes into the maintenance of accurate financial records and reports. There are no specific biblical qualifications for the office of treasurer but there are certain essential duties a treasurer must perform to be effective office holder.

Duties

- maintain updated church financial records
- deposit monies in the bank
- keep a record of church receipts and expenditures
- aids in the procurement of church financial loans
- keep the pastor and trustees posted on the condition of all church assets
- makes financial reports monthly, quarterly, annually whenever necessary
- sign all church expenditures

Chairperson of the Christian Ministry

- assist the ministry in the development of overall goals and objectives for educational program plans
- chairs Christian Education Ministry meetings
- compiles agenda for board meetings.
- makes quarterly/annual reports to the board or the church
- represents the Christian Education Ministry at most of the official church meetings
- helps to supervise and distribute the educational budget of the church
- leads in the development of strategies to address educational needs

Director of Age Group Ministries (Children/Youth/Adults)-

- helps in the recruitment of leaders for ministry with children/youth/adults
- provide educational opportunities
- create an environment of learning
- plan special days and events for children/youth/adults
- makes appropriate use of facilities
- suggest types of educational resources to be used with their specific age group
- supervise Monies budgeted for programs

Director of Children's Ministry-

- advise the church on how to properly address the spiritual and the religious education needs of the children
- assist in the recruitment of program assistants
- advise in the use of program materials, supplies, monies and space
- work with other church leaders in enrolling additional children in church programs
- conduct special training sessions for program assistants
- serve as a role model for all children in the church
- supervise program activities
- prepare an annual youth program budget for recommendation to the finance committee

Director of Youth Work

- advise the church on how to properly address the spiritual and social needs of the youth
- assist in the enlistment of youth program assistants

- advise in the use of program materials, supplies, monies and space
- work with other church leaders in enrolling additional youth
- conduct special training sessions for program assistants
- serve as a role model for all youth in the church
- supervise youth program activities
- prepare an annual youth program budget for recommendation to the finance committee

Missionary Circle Director

- encourages persons to be involved in missions
- organize various mission projects
- develop a comprehensive program plan
- make persons aware of missions
- work with the pastor and church members on mission programs
- encourage teachers and other leaders to study mission materials
- evaluate various mission's programs and determine the use of the mission's offerings
- support state and national missions

Training Union Director

- devise strategies for leadership training
- organize leadership seminars and workshops
- make the congregation aware of leadership materials and publications
- plan for an ongoing program of training for all educational leaders
- keeps the pastor aware of new leadership developments
- conduct planning sessions
- preside over meetings
- plan and supervise a budget for training purposes
- represent and the Training Union during church conference and other meetings
- assist in conducting training
- participate in and promote biblical teaching
- team with the pastor on special projects

Vacation Bible School Director-

- assist in determining school objectives
- choose the type of school

- guide in organizing a VBS calendar
- help choose curriculum
- assist in the selection of VBS workers
- select a good record keeping system
- decide on the best use of facilities
- utilize and evaluate teaching tool

Music Director

- coordinate music within the entire church program
- serve as a representative on the church council
- assist the pastor in planning music for the worship service
- supervise the work of music leaders
- schedule music programs in the church
- conduct music practice sessions
- sponsor music seminars and workshops
- keeps pastor informed on current music trends
- prepare annual budget to be submitted to the Budget Planning Committee

Music is extremely important in a worship service. Musical instruments have been used throughout the history of the church. The Scripture highlights several musical instruments such as trumpets and harps. Psalms 100 says 1Make a joyful noise unto the LORD, all ye lands.

2Serve the LORD with gladness: come before his presence with singing. 3Know ye that the LORD he is God: it is he that hath made us, and not we ourselves; we are his people, and the sheep of his pasture. 4Enter into his gates with thanksgiving, and into his courts with praise: be thankful unto him, and bless his name. 5For the LORD is good; his mercy is everlasting; and his truth endureth to all generations.

Christian Education Resources

Resources

There are basically five types of Christian Education resources. They are listed under the following categories:

A. People Resources:

B. Equipment Resources:

Tablets
Computers
Etc.

C. Financial Resources:

Dollars

Nickels

Quarters

D. Facility Resources:

F. Spiritual Resources:

Prayer
Faith
The Bible
The Holy Spirit

A resource is a spiritual or physical reservoir that can be drawn as an aid in the teaching process. The laity is a very important people resource. There are qualified individuals in most churches who are willing to give of their time and energy to assist in the educational development of the church. The laity is a great educational source which can enhance a Christian education program. Other people resources are found in the following areas:

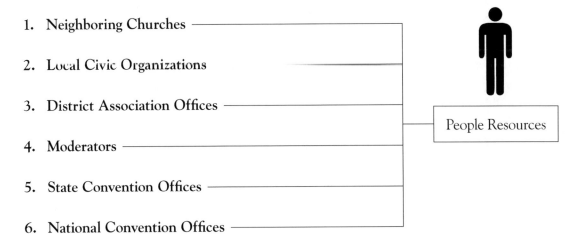

1. **Neighboring Churches**

2. **Local Civic Organizations**

3. **District Association Offices**

4. **Moderators**

5. **State Convention Offices**

6. **National Convention Offices**

People Resources

Church resources are extremely important to the success of the Church and its programs. The churches that have sufficient resources are in a better position of educating and maintaining their membership. Some churches have lost members due to the lack of spiritual and material resources within the Church.

We live in a Social Media world where churches advertise what they have to offer. Advertising educates the public as to what they may be missing in their personal churches. Some of the Social Media promotion entices members to leave a church and join another.

Rather than criticize members for leaving and joining other churches it may be well worth the time to research and find out why members leave. Insufficient spiritual and material resources may be the main reason.

The church should investigate the character and integrity of all resource personalities. Persons selected should be dedicated and have the necessary experience, talents, skills, training and Christian commitment to be effective.

With an increased interest in Christian Education many Christian organizations have increased their supply of material and equipment resources. **The following are examples of Material Resources:**

1. Bibles of diverse types & brands
2. Bible dictionaries & concordances
3. Bible commentaries & handbooks
4. Christian study guides on topical Bible studies
5. Sunday school quarterlies
6. Church program manuals
7. Christian autobiographies
8. Church training manuals
9. Christian education manuals
10. Bible games & flash cards
11. Mission study guides
12. Flip charts & maps

Bible Resources

Equipment Resource

1. iPads
2. LCD Projects
3. Video tapes
4. Overhead projects
5. Compact Disc
6. Blue Ray Players
7. Computers
8. Record players
9. Tablets
10. Musical instruments

Device Resources

Equipment and material resources are aids to teaching. Those who use equipment resources are encouraged to be familiar with the proper use of the resource to maximize its effect on the teaching process.

The church that has a Christian Education Ministry or similar organization would be wise to examine all materials and equipment resources to see that they meet Christian standards. Materials that decentralize the importance of Jesus Christ may be detrimental.

All resources, whether they are people or material should be evaluated periodically to assess its' educational value and cost effectiveness. If the resources do not meet the desired spiritual and educational needs, it is the responsibility of the Christian Education Ministry to act to remedy the problem.

Facility and financial resources are certainly among the most significant resources in a Christian education program. Having sufficient financial resources to purchase educational materials along with having adequate educational space enhances a church's Christian Education program. People tend to learn better in attractive, spacious areas. Everyone needs room for movement and relaxation during a lecture or teaching session.

Many churches have built separate educational buildings for their Christian Education needs. A large number of churches report a significant increase in Christian Education involvement since the addition of the facilities.

Christian Education facilities are normally built to provide educational space for various age groups with future growth projections in mind. Any church that enters a Christian Education building program should have a positive attitude believing that growth will occur and that the space will not be wasted. There are various books available to assist a church in designing an educational facility with future growth in mind.

The Christian Education Ministry has the responsibility of making the church aware that sufficient finances are essential to building a strong Christian Education program. The church, which is well informed on Christian Education matters, can better determine which programs to promote and budget.

If a Christian Education program receives the necessary operating funds, there should be some solid identifiable events and functions which the church recognizes as responsible, caring ministry. When good programming exist, future funding is almost assured.

The Church That Maximizes Christ Centered Resources Will Go Along Toward Building A Sound Christian Education Program

Importance of Time Management

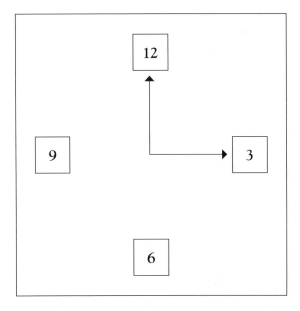

Time management is essential to an effective Christian Education program. Time is a very special commodity, which should not be taken for granted. Every unproductive second cannot be replaced.

Most successful Christian Education programs are time conscious. They schedule meetings at specific times during the week and adjourn the meetings as close to the planned ending time as possible.

Effective Time Management Ideas

- plan and research before scheduled meetings
- practice time management in all phases of life
- avoid excessive scheduling

- be schedule oriented
- live a balance life, between work, recreation and worship
- pray for time consciousness
- have an organized file system; know where materials and resources can be found
- beware of spiritual and social matters
- continue to work toward better time usage
- avoid unnecessary practices

WAYS TO OBSERVE TIME SCHEDULES

Planning Calendar											
Jan.	Feb.	Mar.	Apr.	May	June	July	Aug.	Sept.	Oct.	Nov.	Dec.

- have a well-planned agenda
- limit the discussion to specific areas of importance
- distribute the agenda prior to the meeting
- encourage the Christian Education Committee members to be serious about achieving the goals and the objectives of the Ministry
- encourage members to be on time

Planning Leads to Success

Planning is the key to time management. The lack of planning usually leads to delays and ineffectiveness in Christian Education programming. Christian educators must go a step beyond planning. They must activate their plans by obediently implementing the plans. Planning will not benefit a program if they are not put into action.

Rest and Relaxation Increases Potential Success

Proper rest and relaxation is essential in time management. A clear mind and rested body has a way of inspiring a person to do their best. The effectiveness of a person is greatly reduced when they are in a fatigued state. Each Christian Education Ministry member should make an attempt to be properly rested prior to coming to ministry meetings. Psychological and Physical fatigue simply robs a person of their concentration which leads to wasted time and a lack of accomplishment.

Time Management is Essential

Time management must become a leading priority before it benefits a church or organization. There must be a willingness to make the necessary sacrifices to see that time designated schedules are observed. The observance of Time management aids in the efficiency of church programming. All church organizations are encouraged to exercise proper control to see that time management is a priority.

The Value of Time Management Cannot Be Overstated. It is Essential to Stress the Importance of Making the Best Use of Time.

Age Groups

The psychology of age groups is an area that every person in Christian Education should be aware of. Each age group has its' own individual needs. These needs must be addressed if any genuine Christian Education is to take place.

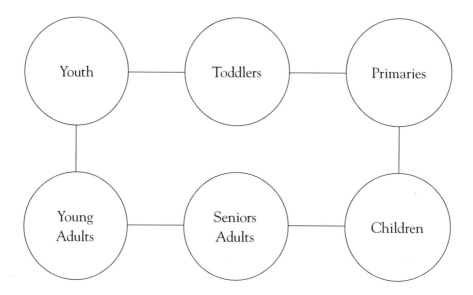

Teachers who possess a knowledge of Age Group Psychology are better equipped to keep and retain the interests level of their pupil.

Knowing the psychological profiles of various age groups is extremely important in the Contemporary Church. Each age group is unique and have specific needs that are germane to that age group.

The teacher who uses a variety of teaching methods have a better chance of maintaining the attention of the students. Each age group need to be instructed in a unique way to maximize their learning experience.

DEVELOPMENTAL STAGES

Growing to Maturity

According to the great Swiss Psychologist Jean Piaget the preschool years (birth to 5) are in the formative years. The foundation of a child's personality is generally formed by the end of these years. In the initial stages of the formative years, the child learns to crawl, talk, walk, use the toilet and respond to their parents, siblings and others. They also learn to trust and distrust through association with their parents and other persons in their environment.

Preschoolers are eager and ready to learn. Workers in Christian Education can create an environment where positive Christian stimuli are transmitted. It is essential to capitalize upon the tender years of a person's life, a period when there is a genuine openness to learning new experiences.

Curiosity is at its most intense level during the formative years of a child's life. Children, during this stage, learn mostly from concrete experiences (things they can feel and touch.) The physical sensitive level is very high in preschool. Pain is intense, joy is genuine. The preschooler's sense of sight, sound, taste and touch are very keen.

Learning experiences during the preschool stage of life should complement the child's senses. Objects such as balls, dolls, clocks and toy trucks and cars can be used in the teaching process. It would be a plus to use bright colorful objects. Every effort should be made to appeal to as many of the child's senses as possible.

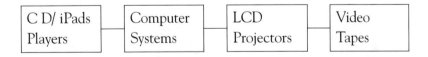

| C D/ iPads Players | Computer Systems | LCD Projectors | Video Tapes |

Audio visuals such as tape recorders, CD players, LCD projectors, etc. can be utilized at the appropriate times to stimulate the child's interests in the learning process. Persons who use audiovisuals should be thoroughly familiar with the aids before using them; misuse of such aids could do more harm than good.

Preschoolers Learn Through Using Their Hands

It is important that all instructors map out strategies in using teaching aids. Sufficient planning time should proceed each teaching session.

In working with preschool children, it is very important to remember that preschoolers learn better when they work with their hands. Teaching experiences which encourages preschoolers to use their hands can be enjoyable for both the teacher and the pupil

Pre School Hand Use Activities:

- Play CD's which require the children to clap their hands& stomp their feet
- Use Bible puzzles
- Use Bible coloring books; supervise the children as they color different Biblical characters
- Read some background information on each Biblical character colored by the child
- Instruct the children to draw pictures of Biblical characters
- Encourage children to print various Bible verses

Allowing preschool children to work with their hands is very beneficial, but it is also very essential that variety be used in the teaching process. Preschoolers have multidimensional personalities; therefore, it is important to use a variety of teaching activities in instructing them. For instance, it would be helpful to use a combination of the following activities in instructing them:

- encourage the preschooler to repeat carefully phrased cheers
- use recreational music
- allow the child to read or sing Christian songs if they desire to do so
- make use of arts and crafts
- have visual presentations
- use puppetry
- encourage the preschooler to memorize short Bible verses
- invite different children to come and share with the group
- go on field trips

Facility

Harry Piland says in his book Basic Sunday School Work that preschoolers are active by nature. Therefore, they need space to move about and develop their minds, bodies and muscles to commensurate with their maturation.[1]

The short attention span and the curious nature of pre -schoolers mandate that they have enough space to explore and learn.

Piland says, "Ideally, preschoolers should have a rectangular shaped room, a room that is three fourths as wide as it is long."[2] Piland goes further to say that the room should be large enough to allow at least 20 feet per child in addition to space needed for teaching aids and resources.[3]

Ideally the room should be sectioned off into neat organized stations with an assistant teacher manning each station.

Toys Arts And Crafts Area	Bible Study and Music Area	Classroom
	Play and Recreation Section	
		Area

Suggested Stations Are:

A. Bible Study and Music Section

B. Toy, Arts and Crafts Section

C. Play and Recreation Section

D. Classroom Section

Teaching Stations

Children need to learn organization at an early age. A properly sectioned learning environment for children would reinforce the significance of being organized and purpose oriented.

In a preschool environment, the promotion of scriptural awareness should be a top priority. Colorful pictures and written Bible expressions could enhance the preschooler's awareness of Jesus Christ and the nature of God; however, it is important that the pictures and expressions be strategically placed where they can easily be used as general teaching resources.

Rooms should not be decorated with too many bold colors, which could distract the child from learning.[4] Piland says that babies, creepers and toddlers need a quiet environment, which is conducive to rest. He says neutral and soft pastels are good wall colors for a calming and relaxing effect on young preschoolers. Soft blue has been found to make infants cry less.[5]

Recess

Rest and Relaxation is Part of the Learning Process

Preschoolers need time to relax and to be themselves at some point during the teaching process. They will respond more positively when sufficient recess time is allowed.

IMPORTANT DATES

Calendar

Thanksgiving, Christmas, Easter, Mother's Day
Father's Day, and Promotion Day

Preschool workers need to be aware of important dates in a child's life.

Some Important Dates Are:

- Birthdays
- Christmas
- Valentines' Day
- Promotion Day
- Easter

- Grandparents' Day
- Mothers' Day
- Fathers' Day
- Awards' Day

These dates need to be emphasized or highlighted on the church school fiscal calendar.

Annual Progress Banquet

Persons working with preschoolers have the option of giving inexpensive gifts on the appropriate occasion, such as Christmas, Easter, Thanksgiving, etc. Monies are normally budgeted for such occasions, but if not, individual sacrifices may be in order.

RECORD AND FINANCIAL RESOURCES

Keep Good Records and Manage Finances

It is very essential that a Preschooler Department keep good records. A registration card, listing each child's name, current address, date and place of birth, names of parents and siblings should be kept in a safe file.

Good organized records of each child are beneficial in case of an emergency. Profile records can also aid in witnessing to unchurched and/or unsaved members of the child's family.

CHILDREN DIVISION Ages 6 - 12 (Grades 1 - 6)

The first stage CHILDREN Ages 6 - 9

The Critical Learning and Socialization Years

Children (age 6-9) learn through concrete experience. They are more concerned with the appearance and the surface dimension of learning than the internal source of learning. They describe life as their eyes see it. People and objects are described as big, small, ugly, pretty, etc. Sophisticated jargon has little place in their vocabulary.

During this time a child becomes more aware of the significance of learning about the world around him. He notices the differences in himself and others, especially the opposite sex. They are more open to socialization than in the past years and begin to see the value of peer and group relationships. Teamwork and group participation is a very rewarding and satisfying thing to a child in this age group.

Increased self-confidence inspires them to share their ideas and opinions. Many children in this age group have special talents in areas such as music and drama. There are times in the teaching process when children who possess special talents could be called on to share their talents with the group.

Learning by doing is very important to the school age child. They are action and experienced oriented. They are impressed with movements, sights, and sounds. Variety is also very important to this age group. They respond more readily to an instructor who modifies his or her teaching style periodically. They learn most effectively when they are challenged with new and rewarding experiences.

CHILDREN - Age 10 - 12

The Humorous Laughing Fun Years

Children in this age group can think abstractly. They can give graphic descriptions of moving experiences. They are more sophisticated than the 6-year-old who learned mostly from concrete experience.

This is also the age group where children tend to learn rapidly and have vivid imaginations. Some have grand ideas about the world and people. They tend to respect the rights of others and are generally less selfish than their preschool counterpart. During this period children generally learn how to deal with failure and success. They are usually very sensitive and strive to do their best in assigned group projects.

Children in the (10 to 12) age range usually have significant questions about life, death, sex and religion. Many times, they seek answers to these questions from Sunday school teachers and religious leaders. Persons involved in Christian Education should be prepared to deal with such questions in a spiritual and intellectual way.

Professions of faith tend to occur in his age range. Children who make professions of faith should be given guidance and support in their spiritual development.

Teachers of children age 10 to 12 can respect their independent nature by allowing them to participate in the teaching process. Children age 10-12 are not to be underestimated, for when given a chance they usually will perform well when they volunteer in the teaching process. But, it is essential that teachers and aids maintain control over the children in this age group and not allow them to take on too much responsibility.

Christian instruction should be administered in a loving, caring manner. Those who work with children or any other age group must never lose sight of the person of Jesus Christ in the teaching process. When teaching materials or teaching methods lead a child away from the significance of Christ as Lord and Savior, it can be very harmful.

THINGS TO REMEMBER IN WORKING WITH CHILDREN

In Memoriam

- assign individual and group projects which will require children to work with their hands.
- encourage children to repeat given cheers and phrases
- give verbal reward when appropriate
- give children an opportunity to demonstrate a given talent if they desire to do so
- listen to what the child has to say
- beware of body language
- use music at various intervals in the teaching process
- allow sufficient recess time

YOUTH

The Questioning Challenging Years

Early Adolescence - Ages 12 to 14 (Grades 6-8)

Adolescence is a transitional period. It is generally a period of mixed emotions. There is the excitement of growing older and wiser but at the same time there is the anxiety of dealing with new physical changes such as the onset of puberty and the strong attraction to the opposite sex.

Adolescence is a critical period of development. Teachers of this age group should be sensitive to the needs of this age group. Only teachers who are controlled by the Holy Spirit and possess gifts in youth ministry should be allowed to work with adolescents for it is generally a period when youth are very keen on hypocritical behavior. They know if a person is genuine or not.

Many times, the decision to follow Christ or to reject Him is made during this period therefore; it is especially important that this age group have positive Christian Role Models to pattern their lives after.

LATE ADOLESCENCE- 15 TO 21

The Opinionated Independent Thinking Years

During this stage of development, youths generally become increasingly more independent in their thinking patterns; some become very opinionated and flout their intelligence to let their peers and superiors know that they have established a trend of thought. Some have acquired a systematic philosophy, which they defend and protect vigorously.

Persons in this age group tend to clarify their value system and sharpen their commitments. Most establish a specific lifestyle, which reflect their overall religious orientation. Those who are Christian will tend to project Christian characteristics and those who are non-Christians will tend to be influenced more by their peers and society more than established religious value systems.

The process of self-identity comes into focus in this age group. A person comes to understand more vividly their strengths, weaknesses, intellectual and physical limitations which enhances their self-esteem.

The adolescent is caught between two worlds; they are neither fully mature adults nor are they little boys or girls. They are in transition from childhood to adulthood, which makes life especially, challenging. Parents, Sunday school teachers, and educators need to be aware of the challenges and influences, which confronts those who are adolescent.

They must remember that adolescence is a temporary stage in a person's growth and development. If the adolescent appears to be uncooperative, moody or arrogant, it may be that he or she is testing their newly found freedom by experimenting to find acceptable behavior patterns which they feel comfortable with.

Those who teach this age group must be aware that at times many transitory thoughts may flow through the mind of the adolescent. There may be questions of academic failure or success, questions of religious values and morality, questions and concerns about the appropriate expression of sex and questions of future marriage and career advancement. Many times, these concerns bombard the adolescent's thinking process and leave them puzzled and confused. Teachers of Christian Education should be open and candid with the adolescent in order that he or she will feel free to come and share their joys and frustrations.

YOUNG ADULTHOOD

First Stage age 21 to 25

The Reality Recognition Years

During the initial stages of young adulthood many persons will have settled into the work world or completed four years of college, and some will have finished two years of graduate school or may be employed in each profession.

Many persons during this stage will have served in the military and will have had their first child; some will have completed their families. Increased responsibility during this stage of life is often a catalysis that causes many young adults to use logic when solving difficult problems rather than to rely solely on emotion or intuition.

Second Stage age 28 to 40

Understanding Less Critical Years

The second stage of young adulthood is age 28 to 40 a stage in life when many vocational decisions are made. Some choose to return to school to get additional education for being more marketable and it is also a stage in life when many choose divorce and separation as a new style of life.

Persons who work with young adults should use materials, which speak to their needs and concerns. It would be helpful to use materials, which address the family, marriage, sex, current events, and Spiritual Concerns; these are areas of study which many young adults find relevant and interesting.

Young Adult Teaching approaches:

- question/discussion
- lecture/discussion
- group projects
- team teaching
- periodical guest speaker

Activities:

- dinner fellowships
- baby contest
- talent contest

Middle Adulthood Ages 40 to 70

The first stage 40 to 54

The Advice-Giving Years

Middle adulthood is generally the longest stage of a person's life. It is a very diversified stage of life. The early years of middle adulthood (ages 40-50) is usually marked by the presence of children attending grade school, high school, and some entering college. Parenthood is generally very challenging during this period Children are growing up and becoming young men and women. It takes a patient, understanding parent to develop a positive relationship with children who are trying to establish their own identity.

Middle Adulthood is usually the period in life when there is a desire to contribute to the next generation. There is generally a realization that time is precious. Options, which were available at a younger age, are no longer available. A change of career, divorce, remarriage, children leaving home are all events that often occur during this stage in life.

The Second Stage of Middle Adulthood

Rational Decision-Making Years

In the late stages of middle adulthood (ages 55-70), aging usually becomes more pronounced. Some persons become self-conscious of the aging process and worry unnecessarily over effects of aging. This is unfortunate because the aging process is a natural process, which affects everyone.

Some persons in this stage rebel against aging by regressing to earlier youthful behavior. It is important that persons in this age group maintain a good relationship with their spouses, children and peers. It is best to accept the process of aging with grace and style for it is a natural process that everyone goes through.

Middle age men and women need to acquire good Prayer and Bible study habits. Unlike children, they usually do not have strong parents to turn to for comfort and guidance.

Teaching Approaches:

- discussion Groups
- well planned questions/answer sessions
- personalized group presentations
- spouse retreats
- character studies

Later Adulthood ages 70 and over

The sharing of wisdom and knowledge years

Later adulthood is usually characterized as an advice-giving stage of life. Most persons in this stage of life have retired and serve as excellent resource persons due to their mature outlook and numerous life experiences.

Persons in this age group have generally settled into a mode of thinking. They have strong convictions and generally maintain their religious beliefs. During this stage of life, adults need to know that their talents are still needed. Teaching activities should incorporate the skills and talents of those in this age group.

This is generally the group, which appreciates the company of children and young people. Many in this age group have grandchildren, which is a source of joy and fulfillment.

There are times when a young person could be called on to aid in the teaching of this age group. A well-prepared young person could be a relief teacher to this group on an occasional basis.

Later adulthood is also a period when one is usually concerned about his or her health. A person's health is usually not as good as it once was; which makes them more susceptible to colds and disease. Their movement is not as swift. Their sight and hearing are not what it once was. Teachers should be sensitive to the needs of this age group and make sure each person is comfortable with selected teaching methods.

The inevitability of death is more pronounced in this age group than it has ever been. During this stage of life companionship is very important. The decreased mobility of this age group often leads to an increase of loneliness because of the lack of socialization. It is important that a Christian Education program provide opportunities where senior citizens can get together and fellowship and share.

Suggested Senior Citizen Activities –

- Lecture/discussion
- Arts and crafts production
- Audio-visual presentation
- Adopted grandchild program
- Group discussion
- Retreats and field trips

All the preceding activities are ways in which senior citizens can enjoy the learning process.

Singles

The singles population in the church should not be overlooked. Many people choose to remain single and many are separated or divorced. Ministries to these groups of people are very essential. They have their own interests, which needs to be properly addressed.

Most Christian publishers produce Sunday School and Church-Training resources especially designed for singles. If a church has a sizable number of singles it may be well worth the churches ' efforts to invest some money in resources designed for singles, divorces, widows and widowers.

Persons who minister to singles should be sensitive to areas of study which addresses singles issues. If the church is large enough, singles should be divided into age groups like those of the standard Sunday school groups.

Suggested Single Group Activities:

- dinner fellowships/group retreats
- joint meetings with other singles from surrounding churches
- current event lectures/group discussions
- question/answer sessions

Singles are a growing demographic in the Contemporary Church. Some singles are divorced. Churches must find ways to effectively minister to singles. A church would benefit from meeting with the singles to get their input as to the kinds of church programs they desire to be involved in. Most Singles have excellent ideas about Church programs and events that would interest them.

Group outings and trips may be an option for singles in today's Contemporary Church. Meeting at the homes of those who volunteer to host various events may be another alternative that may appeal to some singles. It is important to note that Church Singles events should maintain the integrity of the Spiritual teachings of Jesus Christ.

The Art of Ushering

Ushering

Ushering is a very important church function. Those who serve as Ushers are called to one of the most important positions in the Church. Ushers are usually the first church officials to greet visitors. They help set the tone of the worship service. Many times, visitors rate the friendliness of a church on how they were received by the ushers.

I Was Glad When They Said unto Me Let Us Go into the House of the Lord Psalms 122:1

Ushers in the Old Testament were called doorkeepers. They were the doorkeepers of the house of God, the tabernacle, and later the temple. No one could hold a position in the temple or tabernacle unless they were devout temple worshipers. (Psalm 84:1,4,10)

It is important that ushers learn the language of ushering. They need to know the definition of words associated with ushering, the qualifications, the duties and the resources of ushers.

The mood of ushers can impact Church growth; some visitors join churches due to the friendly inviting spirits of ushers. It is important that ushers know how to greet and meet Church members and visitors. First impressions are extremely important in a church setting. Once an impression is made it is difficult to change the perception of a person. It is important that ushers make a good first impression, because they may not get a second chance. No Church wants a reputation of being cold or unfriendly. It is important that ushers be prayed up and project a loving caring spirit.

A. Meaning of Usher

Ushering is a very Noble Christian Service

Webster's dictionary defines usher as a guide.[1] Ushers serve in secular settings such as football games, basketball games, nightclubs, etc. and they serve in religious settings, particularly in churches.

B. Important Words Associated with Ushering

Know the Language of Ushering

Confident- An usher must possess a spiritual and a professional attitude.

Dedication - A person must be willing to work hard if they are to become a good usher. They must perform their duties out of love for a worthy Christian cause. A dedicated usher is a precious servant in the house of God.

Alert – Effective Ushers are observant because it takes exceptional concentration to be a good usher

Courteous - "Common courtesy goes a long way" is a profound statement because courtesy is extremely important in ushering. A good passage of Scripture to remember concerning courtesy is "[12] Therefore all things whatsoever ye would that men should do to you, do ye even so to them: for this is the law and the prophets KJV Matthew **7:12**

All the preceding words are associated with ushering, but the most important word is love. Ushers must possess the love of Jesus Christ to be effective workers in the household of God.

Usher Emergencies Some of these may be:

- urgent phone calls
- illness during the service
- seating shortages
- disturbances by small children
- talker disturbances
- unsupervised children

Emergencies will rise at given times. The best guard against emergencies is to have a chain of command and be prepared to act. Ushers need to practice emergency situations, acquire First Aid Certification, and know the location of telephones and know emergency phone numbers. It is also important that they know how to give emergency personnel clear and concise directions.

Some churches have medical personnel who volunteer their services; this is good, but ushers should also be certified in first aid.

C. Qualification of an Usher

- **Spiritual** - The usher should be a dedicated Christian who is concerned about the up building of the kingdom of God and their lives should reflect the love of Jesus Christ.
- **Physical** - The usher should be physically fit and carry themselves with dignity and grace and practice good posture.
- **Personal Attitude** - The usher should be sound in their judgment and possess a pleasant disposition. They should not allow personal problems to interfere with the performance of their duties.
- **Mental Outlook** – Ushers should possess an optimistic spirit. They should look on the bright side of life. They should be mentally alert and prepared to deal with emergencies during the church services.
- **Personal Appearance**
  - No dangling ear rings
  - Ushers should be neatly groomed
  - Uniforms should be clean and neat and not fit to too tight
  - Uniforms should be below the knees

D. Duties of Ushers

- Make sure that essential resources are ready for the service
- Greet worshipers before and after service
- Seat incoming worshipers at appropriate times during the service
- Distribute church bulletins and service information
- Receive offerings and special gifts

The Sunday School

SUNDAY SCHOOL

Those Who Serve as Sunday School Workers and Teachers
Must Always be Aware That Children Constantly Form
Their Views Through the Actions of Adult Role Models

The importance of the Sunday School to the overall growth and development of the church cannot be overstated. The church, which has a strong Sunday School, is usually a very successful church. Those who attend Sunday school on a regular basis increase their exposure to Christian fellowship and Bible study.

The perceived image of the Sunday School staff, goes a long way in determining a child's perception of Christ and the Church. Children tend to pattern their lives after their teachers and mentors. It is important that all persons who serve in any capacity with the Sunday School are committed genuine Christians who have the child's interest at heart.

The Function of the Sunday School

Character Building and Soul Winning are the Primary Functions of the Sunday School

---

The Sunday School serves a variety of functions, but two of the primary functions are a soul winning agent and a character building organization.

Character building and evangelism are the noblest callings that an organization could have. Those who work with the Sunday School should never take their service for granted because there are too many precious young lives at stake.

The production of upright Christian citizens is essential to a society. The Sunday School, the Church and the family have the greatest responsibility in the Character building of our children.

Sunday School Teachers

Be a Messenger of God's Word, Live a Christian Life in Both Word and Deed

---

Sunday School teachers must not only project a consistent spiritual attitude, but they should also be well organized and punctual. Young people need to be taught the value of organization and the importance of making the best use of their time. The young person who receives positive Christian stimuli in the Sunday School usually excels in other areas of life such as in the home, the school, and in career and social relations.

Selection Process

Look for Teachers Who Possess a Love for Christ and Possess the Intellectual Skills and Spiritual Maturity to Make a Difference in the Lives of Children

---

Christian commitment, character and dedication are qualities to look for in a Sunday school Teacher. The complex world in which we live makes it imperative that the church selects the right persons to serve as teachers. Young people are looking for role models.

Sunday School teachers are among the highest professions that young people model their lives after. A church would do well to be very prayerful, patient and careful in selecting qualified teachers.

The teacher selection process varies from one church to the other. Some churches allow the superintendent to make the selection; others prefer that the pastor initiates all staff changes.

There is no perfect method of selecting a Sunday School teacher, but there is a process, which has worked well in many churches. It is to allow the Sunday School in conjunction with the Ministry of Christian Education to make the selection of teachers with the pastor and church approval.

Length of Service

Traditionally some teachers in smaller churches remain in their positions for life. This may work in some churches but in others it has caused major problems because failure to have a rotating teacher selection process diminishes the opportunity to interject fresh new spiritual ideas into the teaching process. Ideally a rotating teacher selection process would eliminate many of the problems in many churches that have no written policy to deal with teachers who have lost their effectiveness. A teacher rotation process would remind a person that teaching a Sunday School class is not necessarily a lifelong position.

Teachers should not be allowed to stay in positions pass their effectiveness. The work of the Sunday School is too important to be hindered by ineffectiveness. The church, which decides to acquire a rotating teacher system, should fully explain the system before implementing it. Some persons are sensitive when it comes to a teacher rotation process. The teacher who has a clear understanding of the rotation process is better able to accept changes that may occur during the year.

It is entirely up to each individual church as to how often they rotate teachers. Some churches rotate every two or three years. There is no standard system, which is ideal for all churches.

Sunday School Growth

Come to Sunday School. There is a Blessing When We Learn About Christ

Sunday School growth and enlargement involves maintaining the existing enrollment. When a pupil fails to attend Sunday School, a teacher should contact the pupil to let him know that he was missed. A phone call or a visit may be the difference in having a strong viable Sunday School or a weak ineffective Sunday School. Teachers who take the initiative to contact absent pupils usually have a larger and better class attendance.

Sunday school growth is a challenge in the Contemporary Church because there is a lot of competition for the hearts and souls of parents and children. The Social Media and the Multimedia entertainment complex have produced a lot of programs to occupy the minds of people who other wise would attend Sunday School. Perhaps it is time incorporate more technology in teaching Sunday school lessons. There are numerous Technological Christ Centered Resources that have the potential to maintain the attention and interest of youth and children. There is a chance that children would encourage their parents to bring them to Sunday School if the teachers and the resource materials were interesting. When all is said and done never forget the Power of Prayer in aiding the growth and the development of Sunday Schools.

Sunday School – A Family Affair

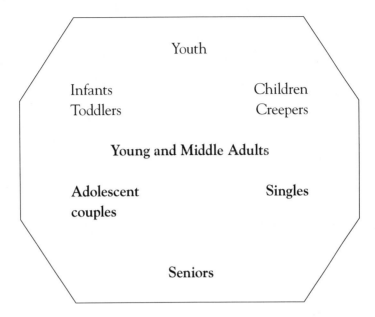

Sunday School is for everyone. The church must overcome the myth that Sunday School is just for children. The truth of the matter is that adults need to attend Sunday School as much as children do. Those who fail to fellowship with other believers and study the bible are subject to live an unfulfilled life. Sunday School provides Christian fellowship and it encourages a person to study the scripture.

Enrollment of the entire church family should be one of the goals of all Sunday School programs. Those who serve on the Sunday School staff should work diligently to find creative ways to promote Sunday School functions.

The best promoters of a program tend to be those who support the organization on a regular basis. The Sunday School Growth Committee should encourage those who attend Sunday School on a regular basis to actively solicit fellow members and unchurched persons to attend Sunday School.

Sunday School is Not Just for Children. The Entire Church Membership Can Benefit from the Teaching Environment of the Sunday School

Jesus Christ trained twelve disciples to spread the message of the gospel. The same approach could be used in a Sunday School, which desires to grow. Dedicated Sunday School members could be trained to be great Sunday School promoters.

Suggestions for Sunday School Promotion

- Printed Posters
- Special Features
- Movies
- Guest speakers
- Written Correspondence
- Oral Announcements
- Enlargement Workshops
- Social Events
- Field trips
- Recreational outings

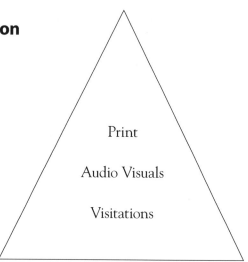

Print

Audio Visuals

Visitations

Leadership and Sunday School Enlistment

Pray for Spiritual Guidance

Leadership is essential to the success of a Sunday School enlistment program. The director of a Sunday School enlistment program should be a sincere dedicated Christian who knows how to organize and knows the value of working with the pastor.

The Sunday School enlistment program, which has the full backing of the pastor, has an ally who can promote the program at key times during the various functions of the church.

Finances and Enlistment

Finances Can Aid in Sunday School Growth and Enlistment

Sufficient financing is another strong ally of the Sunday School enlistment program. The old cliché' that says "money talks" is very true. The Sunday School enlistment program, which has enough money to market and promote its' overall program, stand a good chance of achieving its goals and objectives.

Steps to Increase Enrollment

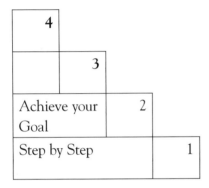

- Pray for guidance of the Holy Spirit
- Work through existing church nomination procedures to appoint
- Start a Sunday School enlistment committee
- Write the State Convention for proven Sunday School enlistment resources
- Write specific enrollment goals and objectives
- Analyze the resources & prayerfully decide on the plan
- Write the resources & prayerfully decide on the best plan
- Audit existing Sunday School records to see who is no longer attending Sunday School
- Seek to enroll all absent parents, all church members, and all unchurched community prospects
- Call and/or visit on a regular basis
- Maintain good records
- Promote the program on a consistent basis

- Periodically re-evaluate the program to see if the goals and objectives are being achieved
- Persist with Godly dedication until all the goals are achieved

Find Ways to Promote the Importance of Sunday School

Sunday School Enlistment and Outreach Ministry

Go into the Highways and By Ways of Life and Compel Men, Women, Boys and Girls to Come to Christ

The Sunday School, which has a strong outreach ministry usually, has a large enrollment. One of the primary purposes of the Sunday School should be to enlist unchurched and unsaved children and adults who live within the target area of the church. Every effort should be made to present the gospel to all persons outside of the church.

Children who are enrolled in the Sunday School may be a prime outreach resource. Many children who attend Sunday School have unchurched and unsaved family members. The enrollment registration card of the child should reflect the church status of the child's parents and siblings. The card should list whether the parents or siblings are churched or unchurched.

The Sunday School, which has an active outreach program, can fulfill the great commission Matthew 28:19-20 (which is to share the good news of Jesus Christ to all persons).

Be Serious About Sunday School Promotion

Keeping Prospects in Sunday School

Good marketing and promotion may get prospects to attend Sunday School but only a good sound Christian program will keep them there.

Ingredients of a good Sunday School Program

Ingredients

- Spirit filled Christian leadership
- Christ centered materials & resources
- adequate building facilities
- sufficient financial resources
- challenging teaching methods
- full support from the pastor
- specific goals and objectives
- patience & endurance
- wisdom of how to build Christian character
- a fervent desire to win souls for Christ

If a teacher is not a good fit or does not have the gifts or talents to teach children, it is very unlikely that the children and youth will be interested in attending Sunday school. The personality, spirituality and the capability of the teacher makes all the difference in having a successful Sunday school. Sunday school teachers who do the same things over and over will get the same results. The need for creative innovative spiritual teachers are at a premium in the Contemporary Church.

A pastor may have to make some difficult choices in approving teacher placement. It is more about the children than it is about the teacher. The Church and the pastor should find ways to energize and promote Sunday school growth and attendance.

Age Group Organization Chart

Preschool
Infants
Babies

Creepers

Toddlers
2 Year Old's
3 Year Old's
4 Year Old's
5 Year Old's

Children
(ages 6-12)
(Grades 1-6)

Younger children
6 (Grade 1)
7 (Grade 2)
8 (Grade 3)
9 (*Grade 4*)
Older Children
10 (Grade 5)
11 (Grade 6)
12 (Grade 7)
18 (Grade 12)

Youth
Early Adolescence
(Ages 13-15)

(Grades 7-9)
13 (Grade 7)
14 (Grade 8)
15 (Grade 9)

Late Adolescence
(First Stage)
(Ages 16-18)
16 (Grade 10)
17 (Grade 11)

Late Adolescence
(Second Stage)
(Ages 19-22)
19 College Freshman
(Second Stage)
20 College Sophomore
(Ages 28-40)
21 College Junior
22 College Senior

Young Adulthood
(First Stage)
(Ages 23-40)

Middle Adulthood
(First Stage)
(Ages 41-55)

(Second Stage)

(Ages 56-69)
Late Adulthood
70 and up

Church Training

Church Training Program

The Holy Bible is the primary training resource

A church training program is needed more now than ever before. Members of a specific church need to know the doctrines and teachings of their church. Many new cults and religions have come on the scene. These groups have targeted established denominations. Many members in established denominational churches are being won over by groups, which stray from traditional Christian doctrine. The only effective way to combat non-Christian teaching is through an established church training program based on the scriptural teachings of Jesus Christ.

Paul says in Galatians 5:17 "For the flesh lusteth against the spirit and the spirit against the flesh and these are contrary the one to the other." (KJV) This scripture magnify the fact that Christians are at war against the forces of Satan. Trained Christian soldiers are needed to march and triumphant over the army of the wicked.

The church which does not have an effective training program is at an extreme disadvantage in maintaining its' membership. As mentioned nontraditional church organizations are actively recruiting members who belong to established Christian churches and they are winning over members in large numbers. The bleeding will only stop when traditional Christian Churches clearly define their Doctrinal positions.

No Christian can afford to take church training for granted. It is only when a person makes a sacrificial commitment to be properly instructed in the teachings of Jesus Christ will they become aware of what it means to be a Christian.

When there is no established church training program, positive intellectual and Christian growth tends to stop. Paul says in II Timothy 2:15 "Study to shew thyself approved unto God, a workman that needeth not to be ashamed, rightly dividing the word of truth." (KJV) These words further magnifies the importance of training and study.

TRAINING DEPARTMENT PERSONNEL

Give the Lord the Best of Your Service

It is important to note that there are only two scriptural offices in the church, namely the pastor and deacons. All other positions in the church are positions of privilege. They are simply positions created by the church to assist in the carrying on of its' business.

Those who serve in positions of privilege are elected by the church body and approved by the pastor and governed by adopted church rules and regulations which are not in conflict with the Bible or the church constitution.

The Director

Be led by the Spirit of Christ

The director under the authority of the church is the top administrative officer of church training. He or she serves within the structure of the Christian Education Ministry. The director oversees planning, promoting, supervising and the execution of the training programs.

The Presiding Officer

Know Church Rules and Regulations and
Administer Them Fairly and Objectively

The director may or may not be the presiding officer.[1] It could possibly be a person designated as president or chairman. There are many options because the director has the right to appoint a presiding officer.

The person who serves as a presiding officer should be familiar with the policies and the structure of the training program. He should also be familiar with parliamentary procedure. The presiding officer should be a fair and honest person. The presiding officer's leadership style could make or break the training session.

Secretary

Stay Organized, Focused and Given to Details

The secretary should keep precise, detailed records of training activities. The records should include the number and types of courses taught, the names of all teachers and the length of time it takes to teach a course.

The secretary is a firsthand assistant to the director. The relationship between the director and the secretary is very important because effective communication saves time and eliminates confusion.

One of the special roles of the church training secretary is to record the minutes during various business sessions. All records such as minutes should be neat and organized and should be stored in a specific location in the church for easy accessibility.

Proficient Grammar, Listening and Communication Skills are Essential in Secretarial Service

The Instructors

Let Your Light Shine So That Others May See Christ Within You

Those who serve, as instructors in the church training program should be committed Christians who have a sense of values and precepts.

Spending sufficient time in study and preparation is very important in all Christian teaching. The instructor should be familiar with his or her course of study. An instructor should know the difference between "transmissive teaching" and "creative teaching. "[2] Transmissive teaching leads a person to commit facts to memory without the benefit of understanding; whereas creative teaching leads a person to apply learning daily with the benefit of understanding and lasting effects.

Seek A True Friend Called "Wisdom"

The Dean

The Dean co-ordinates the entire training effort.[3] Each training union should write their convention to receive the proper forms for the national accreditation of the dean, the instructors and the training union. Most state conventions have resource materials, which can be ordered and used in the training process.

Selection of Training Officers

Pray for Guidance in the Selection Process

Officers are normally elected annually or bi-annually in accordance with the policies and the regulations of the training program.

Planning Committee

Use Good Judgment When Planning

The planning committee is the brain trust of the training program. It is a committee which is either elected or appointed by the director and other church-training officials. It is important that the committee write short, medium and long-range goals to steer the training effort in a specific Christian path.

Committees are encouraged to have specific planning dates within the structure of the training union and it is important that committee members attend district, state and national meetings to keep abreast of new developments and techniques in planning.

Time of Operation

Choose the Appropriate Time for the Maximum Effects

Sunday afternoon is the traditional time when most churches have church training. It is a convenient time for many churches, but no church should feel compelled to have church training on Sunday afternoon, if there is another time slot which is more feasible. The bottom line should be to get maximum participation in a quality Christian training program.

YEAR-ROUND PLAN

Spring	Summer
Fall	Winter

Training in a year around program continues uninterrupted, except for a brief vacation period. This is a good plan, but it is important that the staff get a break to refresh themselves.

SEMESTER PLAN

Semester	Plan

Many churches have incorporated the semester plan, which operates on a similar schedule to the school system. The first semester begins in January, the second in April and the third in September. This schedule leaves July, August, and December open for vacations, planning and evaluating the past year.

An annual commencement service is usually held the third semester. There is usually a banquet/ award ceremony with a guest speaker, or the director delivers an address on past accomplishments and future dreams. Planning and promotion is essential in all major Church Training events.

Church Training is more important in the Contemporary Church than ever before. Jesus was all about teaching and training. In reading the gospels the disciples of Jesus learned from the things he said and did not say and learned from the things he did and did not do. Jesus was all about teaching and training his disciples for a greater cause.

Jesus equipped his disciples to maintain and safe guard the teachings of the gospel which are essential for the salvation of mankind. Jesus was aware that Satan was a crafty adversary whose primary objective is to destroy mankind. Equipping the disciples with the Word was a major goal in the battle against Satan. The Scripture says, "greater is he who lives within you than he who lives in the world." Contemporary Church members need to be taught the Word of God on a continuous basis.

Topics of Study

Teach the Truth of the Scripture

God's Word is Inspiring

All specific areas of study in church training should enhance Christian character. General, areas of study in church training are:

- Evangelism
- Missions
- Christian Doctrine
- Christian Growth
- Family Life
- Church Community
- Leadership

Standard Church Training Areas of Study

Evangelism Missions

Matthew 28:18-20, which is called the Great Commission, magnifies the importance of sharing the good news throughout the world. All genuine Christian programs should emphasize evangelism. It is every Christian's duty to evangelize.

Missions

The entire ministry of Jesus incorporated some phrase of missions. Jesus says in Matthew 25:35 "for when I was an hungered, and ye gave me meat; I was thirsty and ye gave me drink. I was a stranger and ye took me in." (KJV)

Christian Growth

A Christian grows from one degree of grace to another. The quality of training he receives will go a long way in determining how he or she matures as a Christian.

Positive Christian instruction will increase Christian maturity. Negative Christian instruction will inhibit Christian maturity. Christian growth and maturity should be a goal of all Christians. The training program which provides an environment where witnessing, fellowship, bible study and prayer can take place stands a good chance of producing mature Christian servants.

Family Life

The family is under attack more now than ever before. The portrayal of immorality on television, the increase of material prosperity, the devaluation of the sanctity of human life and a decline in genuine Christian worship has influenced many persons to open their lives up to sin and discord.

Ecclesiastes 12:13 says:

"Let us hear the conclusion of the whole matter: Fear God and keep his commandments: for this is the whole duty of man." (KJV)

Christians serve God through showing proper respect toward their husbands, wives, children, relatives and neighbors. Showing respect opens the door to love and unity. When genuine Christian love exists with a family, the family unit will strive and survive.

Children need to grow up in Christian homes. They need direction and guidance in their lives to prepare them for adulthood and future leadership roles. It is important that each family have a system of bible study and that each family member pray for the leadership and guidance of the Holy Spirit.

Families are encouraged to live balanced lifestyles, which incorporate the proper amount of work, play and pray. The Christian life is not always a solemn life of trials and tribulations. Jesus socialized; he went to banquets and marriage feasts. Christians who follow in the footsteps of Jesus are encouraged to find sociable acceptable ways of enjoying the lighter side of life.

Training in family life is essential for a well-balanced family unit. Christians need to be equipped with the strength of the gospel when confronted with satanic attacks on the family.

Church Community

Sharing and fellowshipping in the church and the community is very important. The church must extend into the community and address the needs of the lonely and the disenchanted, and it must strive to minister to the unchurched and to those who do not attend church on a regular basis.

Leadership

Producing Christian leadership is certainly one of the primary objectives of a church training program. No organization can function properly without sound leadership. All Christians can benefit from leadership training because all Christians are called to leadership roles on various levels. The church training program, which provides ample opportunities for leadership training, follows the example of Jesus Christ who gave leadership training to all his original twelve disciples.

The disciples of Jesus learned from the things he said and the things he did not say. Jesus taught his disciples up until the time of his death and resurrection. He taught them that a leader should remain firm, patient and loving in the best of times and the worst of times.

The Word of God Is the Path Way to Salvation and a Guide to Wholesome Healthy Living.

Jesus taught through his words and actions. He was confident and sure of himself. He experienced no identity crises. He knew he was the son of the all wise and the almighty God who created the heavens and the earth.

Qualities of Church Leaders

QUALITIES OF CHRISTIAN LEADERS

Sense of Purpose

Be Firm in your Convictions and Beliefs

All persons who are affiliated with a Christian Education program should have a sense of purpose and direction in life. They should take their salvation serious and possess a powerful desire to share their faith with others. A firm belief in Jesus Christ makes a person more aware of his or her talents, skills and limitations. Knowing one's self is essential in Christian leadership.

Willingness to Learn

Possess a Willingness to Learn from Others

Workers in Christian Education must be aware that learning in God's program is a lifelong challenge. Paul says in II Timothy 2:15 "Study to shew thyself approved unto God, a workman that needeth not to be ashamed, rightly dividing the word of truth." (KJV)

A willingness to learn is imperative. A dull untrained mind is a great disadvantage in Christian Education. The overall educational level of the public has risen drastically over the last few years. People are looking for new innovative challenges to stimulate their minds. The Church must try to meet this challenge. The salvation of the unbeliever and the discipling of the saved is worth the investment of time and effort spent in dedicated study. A willingness to learn is a genuine quality of Christian leaders.

Dedication to God

Serve with Unyielding Love and Dedication

All workers in Christian Education should be sincere born-again Christians. The person who has not accepted Jesus Christ as their personal Lord and Savior cannot serve effectively as a worker in Christian Education. The blind cannot lead the blind. The Spirit of Jesus Christ must live in a person before any genuine Christian ministry can take place.

The worker who is dedicated to Jesus Christ will make the sacrifice to do whatever it takes to promote a Christian Education program. A dedicated worker will work long, difficult hours to achieve goals and objectives. He will "Seek first the Kingdom of God and all of his righteousness." Matthew 6:33 (KJV) because he knows the importance of having the right priorities which means placing God first in all endeavors.

Dedication to God steers a person's attention away from selfish goals and objectives and leads a person to focus their attention on the welfare of others. When Christians address the ministerial needs of others, they are being obedient to the teachings of Jesus.

Realistic Attitude

Know your Strengths and Weaknesses

Leaders in Christian Education should know their strengths and weaknesses. The person who knows himself will capitalize on the things they do well.

When setting goals and objectives, a sense of pragmatism should prevail. Unrealistic goals and objectives could devastate a program. Each church must look at its' personal needs and structure programs, which will address those needs. A realistic attitude saves time and money and prevents unnecessary frustrations.

Integrity

Be Honest and Possess a Trusting, Caring Spirit

Christian Education leaders and workers should be honest, sincere and hardworking servants. Their words should be consistent with their actions. Hypocrisy has no place in the church.

Integrity cannot be taken for granted. It can be easily lost by one major mistake. Once a person loses their integrity, it is very difficult to regain it. The best way to maintain a sense of integrity is to associate with persons who are sincere in their Christian walk and pray for the guidance of the Holy Spirit.

Flexibility

Know When to Accept New Ideas

Life is in a continuous state of change. Persons who do not know how to adjust to change are usually frustrated, unfulfilled individuals.

Leaders and workers in Christian Education should be flexible enough to accept positive changes. Those who are open to innovative ideas will grow and progress. There is an abundance of knowledge and wisdom available to all believers. God is willing to share his wisdom with those who pray and ask for the guidance of the Holy Spirit.

Traditional Christian Beliefs

Table of Contents

God the Father

God is the Source of Creation (Genesis 1:1-20 (KJV)

God created the heavens and the earth. He is the final authority and the supreme ruler of all beings. There is one God who is manifest in three distinct attributes without division of nature, being or purpose.

The God of Abraham, Isaac and Jacob Is One God; Deuteronomy 6: 4-6 (KJV)

4 Hear, O Israel: The Lord our God is one Lord: 5 And thou shalt love the Lord thy God with all thine heart, and with all thy soul, and with all thy might 6 And these words, which I command thee this day, shall be in thine heart.

God Created All Things; Genesis 1:1 (KJV)

1 In the beginning God created the heaven and the earth.

Jesus the Son of God

Jesus is the only begotten Son of God (John 3:16 (KJV)

Jesus is the only begotten Son of God. He is the only path of hope and eternal life. He was born to the Virgin Mary. He was crucified on a cross for the sins of mankind, but he arose from the dead to die no more. He took the sting away from death and the victory away from the grave.

Jesus Grants Salvation; John 3:16 (KJV)

16 For God so loved the world that he gave his only begotten Son, that whosoever believeth in him should not perish, but have everlasting life.

Jesus was Crucified on a Cross; Matthew 27:35 (KJV)

35 And they crucified him, and parted his garments, casting lots: that it might be fulfilled which was spoken by the prophet, they parted my garments among them, and upon my vesture did they cast lots.

Jesus Took the Sting Away from Death and the Victory Away from the Grave; 1 Corinthians 15: 55-57 (KJV)

55 O death, where is thy sting? O grave, where is thy victory? 56 The sting of death is sin; and the strength of sin is the law. 57 but thanks be to God, which giveth us the victory through our Lord Jesus Christ.

Jesus Knew No Sin; 1 John 3:5 (KJV)

5 And ye know that he was manifested to take away our sins; and in him is no sin.

The Holy Spirit (The Spirit of Jesus Christ)

The Holy Spirit is the Spirit of Truth Who Abides Within the Believer Forever John 14: 16 (KJV)

The Holy Spirit is the Spirit of Jesus Christ. He is the comforter who was promised in St John 14: 25-26. He is the Spirit that teaches believers all things and he is received when a person confess with their mouth and believe in their heart that Jesus is Lord and Savior. He is an agent of change, power and salvation.

The Comforter Who Teaches All Things; John 14: 25-26 (KJV)

25 These things have I spoken unto you, being yet present with you. 26 But the Comforter, which is the Holy Ghost, whom the Father will send in my name, he shall teach you all things, and bring all things to your remembrance, whatsoever I have said unto you.

The Holy Spirit Initiates Salvation

When Does One Receive the Gift of the Holy Spirit? Acts 2:38 (KJV)

[38] Then Peter said unto them, Repent, and be baptized every one of you in the name of Jesus Christ for the remission of sins, and ye shall receive the gift of the Holy Ghost.

The Union of God, Jesus and the Holy Spirit

God, Jesus and the Holy Spirit are of one mind and one Spirit and one nature. They are in total agreement in love, peace and joy. There is no division or conflict.

There are three that bear witness in Heaven the Father, the Son and the Holy Spirit; 1 John 5: 6-7 (KJV)

[6] This is he that came by water and blood, even Jesus Christ; not by water only, but by water and blood. And it is the Spirit that beareth witness, because the Spirit is truth. [7] For there are three that bear record in heaven, the Father, the Word, and the Holy Ghost: and these three are one.

Jesus is in Total Agreement with the Father; John 5: 19-24 (KJV)

[19] Then answered Jesus and said unto them, Verily, verily, I say unto you, The Son can do nothing of himself, but what he seeth the Father do: for what things so ever he doeth, these also doeth the Son likewise. [20] For the Father loveth the Son and showeth him all.

things that himself doeth: and he will shew him greater works than these, that ye may marvel.[21] For as the Father raiseth up the dead, and quickeneth them; even so the Son quickeneth whom he will. [22] For the Father judgeth no man, but hath committed all judgment unto the Son: [23] That all men should honour the Son, even as they honor the Father. He that honoureth not the Son honoureth not the Father which hath sent him. [24] Verily, verily, I say unto you, He that heareth my word, and believeth on him that sent me, hath everlasting life, and shall not come into condemnation; but is passed from death unto life.

The Holy Scripture

The Scripture is the Inspired Word of God II Timothy 3:16 (KJV)

The Holy Scripture is the inspired Word of God. The original scriptural manuscripts were written without error. Man's proper relationship with God and his fellowman is outlined in the Scripture.

Scripture Reference: II Timothy 3:16

16. All scripture is given by inspiration of God, and is profitable for doctrine, for reproof, for correction, for instruction in righteousness:

Man

The Word Says Man Was Made Just a Little Lower Than the Angels Psalms 8: 4-5 (KJV)

God created man in his own image Genesis 1: 26-27 (KJV). The first man Adam was placed in the Garden of Eden to care for all the living things in the garden. Adam lived a sinless life before he rebelled against the Word of God. Adam was not a programmed robot he was created as a rational being with the freedom of choice.

The Scripture Says Man is Crowned with Glory and Honor Psalms 8:5 (KJV)

---

²⁶ And God said; "Let us make man in our image, after our likeness: and let them have dominion over the fish of the sea, and over the fowl of the air, and over the cattle, and over all the earth, and over every creeping thing that creepeth upon the earth." ²⁷ So God created man in his own image, in the image of God created he him; male and female created he them. Genesis 1: 26-27

Man Was Formed from the Dust of the Earth; Genesis 2: 6-8 (KJV)

Men and Women are Made of the Same Bone and Flesh Genesis 2:23 (KJV)

---

6 But there went up a mist from the earth and watered the whole face of the ground 7 And the Lord God formed man of the dust of the ground and breathed into his nostrils the breath of life; and man became a living soul. 8 And the Lord God planted a garden eastward in Eden; and there he put the man whom he had formed.

Woman

Man was alone in the Garden of Eden. He had no human companion to commune with. One day when man slept God took a rib from his body and formed Woman who became his companion.

Woman Was Formed from the Rib of Man; Genesis 2: 21-25 (KJV)

²¹ And the Lord God caused a deep sleep to fall upon Adam, and he slept: and he took one of his ribs and closed up the flesh instead thereof; ²² And the rib, which the Lord God had taken from man, made he a woman, and brought her unto the man. ²³ And Adam said, This is now bone of my bones, and flesh of my flesh: she shall be called Woman, because she was taken out of Man.

A Man Should Love His Wife; Genesis 2: 24 (KJV)

²⁴ Therefore shall a man leave his father and his mother, and shall cleave unto his wife: and they shall be one flesh. ²⁵ And they were both naked, the man and his wife, and were not ashamed.

The Whole Duty of Men and Women

The whole duty of Men and Women is to serve God and to go into the highways and by ways of life and compel other men and women to accept Jesus as Lord and Savior.

Ecclesiastes 12:13 (KJV)

[13] Let us hear the conclusion of the whole matter: Fear God, and keep his commandments: for this is the whole duty of man.

The Commandment to Love One Another; 1 John 3: 23-24 (KJV)

The First Marriage Was Instituted in the Garden of Eden Genesis 2:24

[23] And this is his commandment, that we should believe on the name of his Son Jesus Christ, and love one another, as he gave us commandment. [24] And he that keepeth his commandments dwelleth in him, and he in him. And hereby we know that he abideth in us, by the Spirit which he hath given us.

Marriage and Family

According to the Scripture God instituted the first marriage in the Garden of Eden. Marriage is the oldest institution known to man. Genesis 1:27 says that According to the Scripture God created Man in his own image. Man was alone, and it was not good for him to be alone; therefore, according to Genesis 2:21 God caused a deep sleep to fall upon Adam and God took one of Adam's ribs and closed his flesh and formed a woman from his rib. The Scripture says that Adam called his wife Eve because she was the mother of all living. Adam and Eve where as one because they were of the same flesh.

Genesis 2:24 says that a man shall leave his father and his mother and shall cleave unto his wife and they shall be one flesh. Ephesians 5: 28 says that a man should love his wife as much as he loves his own body. When true love is shared between husbands and wives there is a bond that remains strong throughout the duration of the marriage Those whom God join are to share an enduring love which will remain unchanged in times of joy and difficulty. The love between a husband and wife is essential to a healthy marriage relationship and it is the primary factor that with impact the rearing of children within a marriage.

1. Marriage is Between a Man and a Woman; Genesis 2: 23-25

[23] And Adam said, This is now bone of my bones, and flesh of my flesh: she shall be called Woman, because she was taken out of Man. [24] Therefore shall a man leave his father and his mother, and shall cleave unto his wife: and they shall be one flesh.

2. How Long Should a Marriage Last?

(A Marriage Should Last unto the Death of the Husband or Wife): Mark 10: 9-12.

[9] What therefore God hath joined together, let not man put asunder. [10] And in the house his disciples asked him again of the same matter. [11] And he saith unto them, Whosoever shall put away his wife, and marry another, committeth adultery against her. [12] And if a woman shall put away her husband, and be married to another, she committeth adultery.

3. Biblical Reasons for Remarriage

(Death); Romans 7:2

[2] For the woman which hath an husband is bound by the law to her husband so long as he liveth; but if the husband be dead she is loosed from the law of her husband.

(Fornication); Matthew 19: 9

[9] And I say unto you, whosoever shall put away his wife, except it be for fornication, and shall marry another committeth adultery: and whoso marrieth her which is put away doth commit adultery.

4. The Benefits of Marriage

- Those who maintain their marriage vows are protected against sexually transmitted diseases
- A happy marriage protects the welfare of the children
- Those who communicate in marriage guard against loneliness and despair

- Those who are happily married live more productive lives
- Marriage is the institution which God ordains the birth of children

5. The Order of Marriage and Children

- Pray for a Christian husband or wife
- Be employed on a job which pays enough to support a Family
- Make sure you are in the will of God
- Make sure you can afford a family before you start one
- During the marriage pray and communicate with your spouse

Sin

The Devil is the Source of Sin I John 3: 8 (KJV)

Sin is the falling short of the standard of God (Theologians say that the standard of God is his laws and percepts.) Adam the first man and Eve the first woman sinned when they rebelled against the laws of God. The Scripture says that there were two trees in the garden: the tree of life and the tree of good and evil. God commanded Adam and Eve not to eat of the tree in the mist of the garden which was the tree of good and evil (which was called the tree of knowledge) Eve was tempted by the serpent. The serpent who represented evil told Eve that God did not want her to eat of the tree because she would be just like God if she ate of the tree. Eve ate of the tree of Good and Evil and shared the fruit of the tree with Adam which was a direct rebellion against God's commandment. Soon after rebelling against the Law of God, Adam and Eve were cast out of the Garden of Eden.

Scripture Reference on Sin

Sin Entered into the World by One Man; Roman 5: 12-19 (KJV)

[12] Wherefore, as by one man sin entered into the world, and death by sin; and so death passed upon all men, for that all have sinned: [13] (For until the law sin was in the world: but sin is not

imputed when there is no law. [14] Nevertheless death reigned from Adam to Moses, even over them that had not sinned after the similitude of Adam's transgression, who is the figure of him that was to come. [15] But not as the offence, so also is the free gift. For if through the offence of one many be dead, much more the grace of God, and the gift by grace, which is by one man, Jesus Christ, hath abounded unto many. [16] And not as it was by one that sinned, so is the gift: for the judgment was by one to condemnation, but the free gift is of many offences unto justification. [17] For if by one man's offence death reigned by one; much more they which receive abundance of grace and of the gift of righteousness shall reign in life by one, Jesus Christ.) [18] Therefore as by the offence of one judgment came upon all men to condemnation; even so by the righteousness of one the free gift came upon all men unto justification of life. [19] For as by one man's disobedience many were made sinners, so by the obedience of one shall many be made righteous.

The Penalty of Sin

Adam and Eve lost their innocence and acquired a sense of guilt and shame. Adam was sentenced to tilling the ground by the sweat of his brow and Eve was sentenced to pain in childbirth. Both Adam and Eve were casted out of the garden and physical death was the consequence of their sin.

Scripture on the Penalty of Sin; Genesis 3: 1-17 (KJV)

[1] Now the serpent was more subtle than any beast of the field which the Lord God had made. And he said unto the woman, Yea, hath God said, Ye shall not eat of every tree of the garden? [2] And the woman said unto the serpent, We may eat of the fruit of the trees of the garden: [3] But of the fruit of the tree which is in the midst of the garden, God hath said, Ye shall not eat of it, neither shall ye touch it, lest ye die. [4] And the serpent said unto the woman, Ye shall not surely die: [5] For God doth know that in the day ye eat thereof, then your eyes shall be opened, and ye shall be as gods, knowing good and evil. [6] And when the woman saw that the tree was good for food, and that it was pleasant to the eyes, and a tree to be desired to make one wise, she took of the fruit thereof, and did eat, and gave also unto her husband with her; and he did eat. [7] And the eyes of them both were opened, and they knew that they were naked; and they sewed fig leaves together, and made themselves aprons. [8] And they heard the voice of the Lord God walking in the garden in the cool of the day: and Adam and his wife hid themselves from the presence of the Lord God amongst the trees of the garden. [9] And the Lord God called unto Adam, and said unto him, Where art thou? [10] And he said, I heard thy voice in the garden, and I was afraid, because I was naked; and I hid myself. [11] And he said, Who told thee that thou wast naked? Hast thou eaten of the tree, whereof I commanded thee that thou shouldest not eat? [12] And the

man said, The woman whom thou gavest to be with me, she gave me of the tree, and I did eat.[13] And the Lord God said unto the woman, What is this that thou hast done? And the woman said, The serpent beguiled me, and I did eat.[14] And the Lord God said unto the serpent, Because thou hast done this, thou art cursed above all cattle, and above every beast of the field; upon thy belly shalt thou go, and dust shalt thou eat all the days of thy life: [15] And I will put enmity between thee and the woman, and between thy seed and her seed; it shall bruise thy head, and thou shalt bruise his heel.[16] Unto the woman he said, I will greatly multiply thy sorrow and thy conception; in sorrow thou shalt bring forth children and thy desire shall be to thy husband, and he shall rule over thee. [17] And unto Adam he said, because thou hast hearkened unto the voice of thy wife, and hast eaten of the tree, of which I commanded thee, saying, Thou shalt not eat of it: cursed is the ground for thy sake; in sorrow shalt thou eat of it all the days of thy life.

The Universal Nature of Sin

All men who are born of a woman are born with a sin nature that can only be redeemed through accepting Jesus Christ as Lord and Savior.

The scripture on the universal nature of sin Romans 3:23 For we all have sinned and come short of the glory of God.

Hell is a Place of Punishment and Separation from God Matthew 13:42 (KJV)

Hell

Hell is a place of eternal suffering prepared for Satan and his demons and for those who fail to accept Jesus

Christ and as Lord and Savior. It is also a place of separation from God.

The Pain of Hell; Matthew 13: 40-42 (KJV)

⁴⁰ As therefore the tares are gathered and burned in the fire; so shall it be in the end of this world. ⁴¹ The Son of man shall send forth his angels, and they shall gather out of his kingdom all things that offend, and them which do iniquity; ⁴² And shall cast them into a furnace of fire: there shall be wailing and gnashing of teeth.

Those Who Are Not Found in the Book of Life Will Be Casted into the Lake of Fire; Revelations 20:10 & 15 (KJV)

¹⁰ And the devil that deceived them was cast into the lake of fire and brimstone, where the beast and the false prophet are, and shall be tormented day and night for ever and ever. ¹⁵ And whosoever was not found written in the book of life was cast into the lake of fire.

The Wicked Will Enter into Hell; Psalm 9: 17 (KJV)

¹⁷ The wicked shall be turned into hell, and all the nations that forget God.

Unbelievers Will Enter into Hell; Revelation 21:8 (KJV)

⁸ But the fearful, and unbelieving, and abominable, and murderers, and whoremongers, and sorcerers, and idolaters, and all liars, shall have their part in the lake which burneth with fire and brimstone: which is the second death.

Heaven is a Place of Eternal Happiness and Peace Revelations 7: 9-14

Heaven

Heaven is the eternal resting placing of the righteous (those who accept Jesus Christ as their Lord and Savior.) It is a place of eternal peace and happiness.

Who Shall Enter the Kingdom of Heaven? Matthew 5:3 (KJV)

³ Blessed are the poor in spirit: for theirs is the kingdom of heaven.

Those Who are Persecuted for Righteous Sake: Matthew 5:12 (KJV)

¹² Rejoice and be exceeding glad: for great is your reward in heaven: for so persecuted they the prophets which were before you.

Those Who Do the Will of God; Matthew 7:21 (KJV)

²¹ Not everyone that saith unto me, Lord, Lord, shall enter into the kingdom of heaven; but he that doeth the will of my Father which is in heaven.

Materialism Can Be a Stumbling Block to Entering Heaven; Matthew 19: 23-30 (KJV)

²³ Then said Jesus unto his disciples, Verily I say unto you, That a rich man shall hardly enter into the kingdom of heaven. ²⁴ And again I say unto you, It is easier for a camel to go through the eye of a needle, than for a rich man to enter into the kingdom of God. ²⁵ When his disciples heard it, they were exceedingly amazed, saying, Who then can be saved? ²⁶ But Jesus beheld them, and said unto them, With men this is impossible; but with God all things are possible. ²⁷ Then answered Peter and said unto him, Behold, we have forsaken all, and followed thee; what shall we have therefore? ²⁸ And Jesus said unto them, Verily I say unto you, That ye which have followed me, in the regeneration then the Son of man shall sit in the throne of his glory, ye also shall sit upon twelve thrones, judging the twelve tribes of Israel. ²⁹ And every one that hath forsaken houses, or brethren, or sisters, or father, or mother, or wife, or children, or lands, for my name's sake, shall receive a hundredfold, and shall inherit everlasting life. ³⁰ But many that are first shall be last; and the last shall be first.

Salvation

Freedom from the Bondage of Sin Luke 4:18 (KJV)

Traditional Christianity Teach That There are Five Stages of Salvation

First, the Holy Spirit (which is the Spirit of Jesus Christ) initiates the salvation process. The following stages highlight the order of the salvation.

A. Repentance

According to Vine's Complete Expository Dictionary the Greek verb for repentance is metametomai it means to regret or to be remorseful. The first stage of receiving salvation is repentance which is a genuine feeling of remorse and a willingness to turn away from sin.

Scripture on Repentance

Ezekiel 18:30 (KJV)

[30] Therefore I will judge you, O house of Israel, everyone according to his ways, saith the Lord God. Repent, and turn yourselves from all your transgressions; so, iniquity shall not be your ruin.

II Corinthians 7:9-10 (KJV)

[9] Now I rejoice, not that ye were made sorry, but that ye sorrowed to repentance: for ye were made sorry after a godly manner, that ye might receive damage by us in nothing.[10] For godly sorrow worketh repentance to salvation not to be repented of: but the sorrow of the world worketh death.

Act 2:38(KJV)

38 hen Peter said unto them, Repent, and be baptized every one of you in the name of Jesus Christ for the remission of sins, and ye shall receive the gift of the Holy Ghost.

B. Confession and Belief

The Greek verb for confession is homologeo which means to declare, to admit or to agree with and the Greek verb for Believe is aman and it means to be firm, endure, stand fast in the truth. The scripture says confess with your mouth and believe in your heart that Jesus is Lord and Savior and you shall receive the Holy Spirit.

Confession and Belief Scripture; Romans 10: 9-11

[9] That if thou shalt confess with thy mouth the Lord Jesus, and shalt believe in thine heart that God hath raised him from the dead, thou shalt be saved. [10] For with the heart man believeth unto righteousness; and with the mouth confession is made unto salvation. [11] For the scripture saith, Whosoever believeth on him shall not be ashamed.

C. Regeneration

The Greek word for regeneration is palingenesia which means rebirth. Spiritual rebirth is the acceptance of Jesus Christ as Lord and Savior, (to be justified (made right with God) to be redeemed from the bondage of sin.

Regeneration Scripture; John 3:3 (KJV)

[3] Jesus answered and said unto him, Verily, verily, I say unto thee, Except a man be born again, he cannot see the kingdom of God.

John 3:16 (KJV)

[16] For God so loved the world, that he gave his only begotten Son, that whosoever believeth in him should not perish, but have everlasting life.

Titus 3: 4-7 (KJV)

[4] But after that the kindness and love of God our Savior toward man appeared, [5] Not by works of righteousness which we have done, but according to his mercy he saved us, by the washing of regeneration, and renewing of the Holy Ghost; [6] Which he shed on us abundantly through

Jesus Christ our Savior; [7] That being justified by his grace, we should be made heirs according to the hope of eternal life.

D. Sanctification

The Greek noun for the word sanctification is hagiasmos and it means a separation to God. Sanctification is the process of growing to Christian Maturity by separating from the ways of the world. It is initiated by the Holy Spirit and enhanced through prayer, bible study, obedience to the Word of God, fellowship with other Christians and resistance to sin and temptation.

Sanctification Scripture; I Corinthians 6: 11 (KJV)

11 And such were some of you: but ye are washed, but ye are sanctified, but ye are justified in the name of the Lord Jesus, and by the Spirit of our God.

John 17:19 (KJV)

[19] And for their sakes I sanctify myself, that they also might be sanctified through the truth.

E. Glorification

The Greek word for glorify is doxazo and it means to praise or to honor. Glorification is the final stage of salvation the process of going home to be with the lord; the receiving of the crown of glory, dwelling in heaven with Jesus. The stage of salvation where perfection is reached.

Glorification Scripture; John 7:39 (KJV)

[39] (But this spake he of the Spirit, which they that believe on him should receive: for the Holy Ghost was not yet given; because that Jesus was not yet glorified.)

The Glorification of Believers; Romans 8: 16-18 (KJV)

[16] The Spirit itself beareth witness with our spirit, that we are the children of God: [17] And if children, then heirs; heirs of God, and joint-heirs with Christ; if so be that we suffer with him,

that we may be also glorified together. [18] For I reckon that the sufferings of this present time are not worthy to be compared with the glory which shall be revealed in us.

The Crown of Righteousness After Physical Death; II Timothy 4: 6-8 (KJV)

[6] For I am now ready to be offered, and the time of my departure is at hand. [7] I have fought a good fight, I have finished my course, I have kept the faith: [8] Henceforth there is laid up for me a crown of righteousness, which the Lord, the righteous judge, shall give me at that day: and not to me only, but unto all them also that love his appearing.

Vine's Complete Expository Dictionary was used as a resource for all the Greek salvation terms.

The Church

There is Power in Prayer and Fellowship Acts 2:42 (KJV)

The New Testament church is composed of baptized believers who have been saved through the grace of Jesus Christ. They are united in love and peace through the Holy Spirit.

The Gates of Hell Shalt Not Prevail Against the Church

Matthew 16: 15-18 (KJV)

[15] He saith unto them, But whom say ye that I am? [16] And Simon Peter answered and said, Thou art the Christ, the Son of the living God. [17] And Jesus answered and said unto him, Blessed art thou, Simon Barjona: for flesh and blood hath not revealed it unto thee, but my Father which is in heaven.[18] And I say also unto thee, That thou art Peter, and upon this rock I will build my church; and the gates of hell shall not prevail against it.

The Early Church Grew and Believers Remained Steadfast in the Apostles Doctrine; Act 2: 38-42 (KJV)

[38] Then Peter said unto them, Repent, and be baptized every one of you in the name of Jesus Christ for the remission of sins, and ye shall receive the gift of the Holy Ghost. [39] For the promise is unto you, and to your children, and to all that are afar off, even as many as the Lord our God shall call. [40] And with many other words did he testify and exhort, saying, save yourselves from this untoward generation. [41] Then they that gladly received his word were baptized: and the same day there were added unto them about three thousand souls. [42] And they continued steadfastly in the apostles' doctrine and fellowship, and in breaking of bread, and in prayers.

Fellowship and Worship in the Church; Act 2: 46-47 (KJV)

[46] And they, continuing daily with one accord in the temple, and breaking bread from house to house, did eat their meat with gladness and singleness of heart, [47] Praising God, and having favour with all the people. And the Lord added to the church daily such as should be saved.

Baptism

Baptism is a Righteous Act of Obedience Which Signals Spiritual Birth into the Kingdom of God (Matthew 3:13-17 (KJV)

The act of Baptism symbolizes the burial of man's sinful nature and the rebirth of a new nature in Jesus Christ. Baptism is viewed as a righteous act because Jesus was baptized, and he commanded his disciples to go into the world and baptize men and women in the name of the Father, the Son and the Holy Ghost. Full immersion is the most common method of Baptism.

The Great Commission of the Church: Go into All of the World and Teach and Baptize All Nations in the Name of the Father, the Son and the Holy Spirit; Matthew 28: 18-20 (KJV)

[18] And Jesus came and spake unto them, saying, All power is given unto me in heaven and in earth.[19] Go ye therefore, and teach all nations, baptizing them in the name of the Father, and

of the Son, and of the Holy Ghost: [20] Teaching them to observe all things whatsoever I have commanded you: and, lo, I am with you alway, even unto the end of the world. Amen.

Jesus was Baptized by John the Baptist; Matthew 3: 13-17 (KJV)

[13] Then cometh Jesus from Galilee to Jordan unto John, to be baptized of him. [14] But John forbad him, saying, I have need to be baptized of thee, and comest thou to me? [15] And Jesus answering said unto him, Suffer it to be so now: for thus it becometh us to fulfill all righteousness. Then he suffered him.[16] And Jesus, when he was baptized, went up straightway out of the water: and, lo, the heavens were opened unto him, and he saw the Spirit of God descending like a dove, and lighting upon him: [17] And lo a voice from heaven, saying, This is my beloved Son, in whom I am well pleased.

Baptism Symbolizes the New Birth; Roman 6: 3-4 (KJV)

[3] Know ye not that so many of us as were baptized into Jesus Christ were baptized into his death? [4] Therefore we are buried with him by baptism into death: that like as Christ was raised up from the dead by the glory of the Father, even so we also should walk in newness of life.

The Spirit of Jesus Confirms Baptism; I Corinthians 12: 13 (KJV)

[13] For by one Spirit are we all baptized into one body, whether we be Jews or Gentiles, whether we be bond or free; and have been all made to drink into one Spirit.

The Lord's Supper

The Lord's Supper is Observed in Remembrance of the Supreme Sacrifice Jesus Christ made on the Cross (I Corinthians 11: 17-28 (KJV)

The Lord's Supper is a symbolic act of obedience observed in accordance to the supreme sacrifice Jesus Christ made on the cross of Calvary. The wine is symbolic of the shed blood of Jesus Christ and the bread is symbolic of his broken body. The Lord's Supper remains us of the pain and the suffering of Jesus on the cross for the salvation of dying men and women; The Lord's Supper is also an expression of fellowship among Christians. Believers who partake of the Lord's Supper are to observe the ordinance in remembrance of the sacrifice Jesus made on the cross. The scripture says that those who observe the Lord's Supper need to examine themselves to make sure that they do not have an offense against their brother.

Scripture on the Lord's Supper; I Corinthians 11: 20-30 (KJV)

[20] When ye come together therefore into one place, this is not to eat the Lord's supper. [21] For in eating everyone taketh before other his own supper: and one is hungry, and another is drunken. [22] What? have ye not houses to eat and to drink in? or despise ye the church of God, and shame them that have not? What shall I say to you? Shall I praise you in this? I praise you not. [23] For I have received of the Lord that which also I delivered unto you, That the Lord Jesus the same night in which he was betrayed took bread: [24] And when he had given thanks, he brake it, and said, Take, eat: this is my body, which is broken for you: this do in remembrance of me. [25] After the same manner also he took the cup, when he had supped, saying, This cup is the new testament in my blood: this do ye, as oft as ye drink it, in remembrance of me. [26] For as often as ye eat this bread, and drink this cup, ye do shew the Lord's death till he come. [27] Wherefore whosoever shall eat this bread, and drink this cup of the Lord, unworthily, shall be guilty of the body and blood of the Lord. [28] But let a man examine himself, and so let him eat of that bread, and drink of that cup.

Forgive your Brother and Sister Before Partaking of the Lord's Supper: I Corinthians 11: 29-30 (KJV)

[29] For he that eateth and drinketh unworthily, eateth and drinketh damnation to himself, not discerning the Lord's body. [30] For this cause many are weak and sickly among you, and many sleep.

The Last Day Teachings

There Will be Trials and Tribulations Before the Return of Jesus (Mark 8: 13 (KJV)

Jesus taught his disciples about the last days and that the world as we know it will come to an end and a new kingdom will be ushered in. Events preceding the second coming of Jesus are highlighted in the scripture. In Mark 13 (KJV) Jesus mentioned the destruction of the temple in Jerusalem. Some scholars believe that the destruction of the temple occurred during the first century other scholars believe that a new temple will be constructed in Jerusalem and the eventual destruction of the new temple will signal the second coming of Jesus.

Scripture on the Destruction of the Temple; Mark 13:1-6 (KJV)

[1] And as he went out of the temple, one of his disciples saith unto him, Master, see what manner of stones and what buildings are here! [2] And Jesus answering said unto him, Seest thou these great buildings? there shall not be left one stone upon another, that shall not be thrown down. [3] And as he sat upon the Mount of Olives over against the temple, Peter and James and John and Andrew asked him privately, [4] Tell us, when shall these things be? and what shall be the sign when all these things shall be fulfilled? [5] And Jesus answering them began to say, Take heed lest any man deceive you: [6] For many shall come in my name, saying, I am Christ; and shall deceive many.

There Will Be Wars and Rumors of Wars; Mark 13: 7 (KJV)

[7] And when ye shall hear of wars and rumors of wars, be ye not troubled: for such things must needs be; but the end shall not be yet.

There Will Be Natural Disasters and Famines and a Multitude of Sorrow and Sadness: Mark 13: 8 (KJV)

[8] For nation shall rise against nation, and kingdom against kingdom: and there shall be earthquakes in diver's places, and there shall be famines and troubles: these are the beginnings of sorrows.

The Gospel Must Be Published Among All Nations Before the End Will Come; Mark 13: 10-11 (KJV)

[10] And the gospel must first be published among all nations. [11] But when they shall lead you, and deliver you up, take no thought beforehand what ye shall speak, neither do ye premeditate: but whatsoever shall be given you in that hour that speak ye: for it is not ye that speak, but the Holy Ghost.

The institution of marriage and the family will be under attack. Brothers will betray brothers and children revolt against their parents. There will be a spirit of rebellion and spirit of disrespect for parental and civil authority. Mark 13: 12 (KJ

A Spirit of Lawlessness; Mark 13: 12 (KJV)

12 Now the brother shall betray the brother to death, and the father the son; and children shall revolt against their parents and shall cause them to be put to death.

A Disrespect for the Sacred; Mark 13; 13-14 (KJV)

13 And ye shall be hated of all men for my name's sake: but he that shall endure unto the end, the same shall be saved. 14 But when ye shall see the abomination of desolation, spoken of by Daniel the prophet, standing where it ought not, (let him that readeth understand,) then let them that be in Judaea flee to the mountains:

An Increase in Suffering and Pain; Mark 13:15-27 (KJV)

15 And let him that is on the housetop not go down into the house, neither enter therein, to take anything out of his house: 16 And let him that is in the field not turn back again for to take up his garment.17 But woe to them that are with child, and to them that give suck in those days! 18 And pray ye that your flight be not in the winter. 19 For in those days shall be affliction, such as was not from the beginning of the creation which God created unto this time, neither shall be. 20 And except that the Lord had shortened those days, no flesh should be saved: but for the elect's sake, whom he hath chosen, he hath shortened the days. 21 And then if any man shall say to you, Lo, here is Christ; or, lo, he is there; believe him not: 22 For false Christs and false prophets shall rise, and shall shew signs and wonders, to seduce, if it were possible, even the elect. 23 But take ye heed: behold, I have foretold you all things. 24 But in those days, after that tribulation, the sun shall be darkened, and the moon shall not give her light, 25 And the stars of heaven shall fall, and the powers that are in heaven shall be shaken. 26 And then shall they see the Son of man coming in the clouds with great power and glory. 27 And then shall he send his angels and shall gather together his elect from the four winds, from the uttermost part of the earth to the uttermost part of heaven.

The Second Coming of Christ

Jesus Will Return in Power and Glory (Luke 17: 24 (KJV)

God will consummate history within his own time. Jesus will return in glory in a visible fashion. The dead will be raised. Christ will separate the righteous from the unrighteous. The scripture says every knee shall bow and every tongue shall confess that Jesus is Lord. The righteous will receive a heavenly reward the unrighteous will be doomed to hell.

Jesus Will Visibly Return in Glory; Matthew 16: 26-28 (KJV)

26 For what is a man profited, if he shall gain the whole world, and lose his own soul? or what shall a man give in exchange for his soul? 27 For the Son of man shall come in the glory of his Father with his angels; and then he shall reward every man according to his works. 28 Verily I say unto you, there be some standing here, which shall not taste of death, till they see the Son of man coming in his kingdom.

When Jesus Return He Will Separate the Saved and the Unsaved: Matthew 25: 31-34 (KJV)

31 When the Son of man shall come in his glory, and all the holy angels with him, then shall he sit upon the throne of his glory: 32 And before him shall be gathered all nations: and he shall separate them one from another, as a shepherd divideth his sheep from the goats: 33 And he shall set the sheep on his right hand, but the goats on the left. 34 Then shall the King say unto them on his right hand, Come, ye blessed of my Father, inherit the kingdom prepared for you from the foundation of the world.

Every Knee Will Bow and Every Tongue Will Confess to God on the Day of Judgment; Roman 14: 11-14 (KJV)

11 For it is written, As I live, saith the Lord, every knee shall bow to me, and every tongue shall confess to God. 12 So then every one of us shall give account of himself to God. 13 Let us not therefore judge one another anymore: but judge this rather, that no man put a stumbling block or an occasion to fall in his brother's way. 14 I know, and am persuaded by the Lord Jesus, that there is nothing unclean of itself: but to him that esteemeth anything to be unclean, to him it is unclean.

How to Remain Christian in an Unchristian Environment

Dr. Emmanuel L. McCall Former Director of the Cooperative Ministries Division of the Southern Baptist Convention was the inspiration behind the writing of this page.

Major Factors in the Life of Jesus Christ:

- Jesus Christ had no identity crisis; He knew he was the son of God.
- Jesus Christ knew his purpose in life; he came to give hope and salvation to dying men and women.
- He remained obedient unto death; he obeyed the word of God.
- He showed genuine love and compassion toward all mankind.

Knowledge to Be Aware of in Your Walk with Jesus:

- be filled with the Holy Spirit
- be prepared to do spiritual battle with the forces of evil
- be aware of your spiritual heritage; you are a child of God
- believe in God; have faith that good will overcome evil

Factors That Contribute to the Filling of the Holy Spirit:

- hunger and thirst for righteousness
- the confession of sins
- willingness to surrender the control of your life to Christ

Things to Do to Remain Strong in the Faith

- pray for the guidance of the Holy Spirit
- study the word of God-memorize key scripture
- fellowship with other believers
- witness with your words and actions
- resist temptation
- take a stand against evil
- forgive those who wrong you- ask others to pray for you

LOVE THOU NEIGHBOR

John 15:12 This is my commandment, that ye love one another, as I have loved you (KJV)

Jesus mentioned love more than any other subject. The nature of God is built upon the foundation of his mercy and love.

St. John 3:16 says: "For God so loved the world, that he gave his only begotten Son, that whosoever believeth in him should not perish, but have everlasting life." (KJV)

Love means responding to the teachings of Jesus Christ in a sincere, positive manner by doing for others when they cannot do for themselves, giving water to the thirsty, feeding the hungry, visiting the sick and the shut-in are examples of sharing love through action.

Love also means the denial of television time, or whatever that gives pleasure, for spending more meaningful time in Prayer and Bible study and it also means spending quality time with children and older people, or the sharing of one's time with persons who have special needs.

Love will inspire a person to share the good news of Jesus Christ with dying men and women for the love of God is sensitive to the wellbeing of others. Love should be extended to everyone. A husband should love his wife and a wife should love her husband. Parents should love their children and children should love their parents. There should be love between brothers and sisters and love among all races and nationalities.

A good bible study plan will aid a person in understanding the biblical principles of love. Paul gives some very interesting insights of love in the 13th. Chapter of first Corinthians, Jesus made a profound statement about love in St. John 3:16 were he says, "For God so loved the world that he gave his only begotten Son that whosoever believeth in him should not perish but have everlasting life". Other highlights of God's love are recorded in the Beatitudes found in the 5th. Chapter of Matthew. Christians are encouraged to read these passages of Scripture and apply them to their daily lives.

THOU SHALT FORGIVE

> Ephesians 4:32 And be ye kind to one another, tenderhearted, forgiving one another, even as God for Christ's sake hath forgiven you. (KJV)

One of the most important lessons Jesus taught his disciples was that they were to forgive their fellow man. Jesus spent a substantial portion of his ministry teaching about forgiving. Jesus says in Matthew 6:14-15: "For if ye forgive men their trespasses, your heavenly Father will also forgive you: But, if ye forgive not men their trespasses, neither will your Father forgive your trespasses." (KJV)

Jesus was sincere in his teachings of the importance of forgiving. Persons who fail to heed his teachings on forgiving goes directly against Christian values and ethics. Jesus instructed his disciples to forgive their fellow man with no limitations.

Matthew 18:21-22 says: "Then came Peter to him and said, Lord, how oft shall my brother sin against me, and I forgive him? till seven times?.Jesus saith unto him, I say not unto thee, until seven times, but until seventy times seven." (KJV) The Hebrews looked upon seven as being a perfect number. The Bible says that God created the world in 6 days and that he rested on the seventh day. Peter thought there was a limit to the number of times a man should forgive his brother. Jesus corrected Peter by saying there are no limits to the number of times a man should forgive his brother.

The person who sincerely forgives his brother will forget the pass transgressions of his brother and seek no personal revenge against him. The spirit of forgiveness is one of the highest Christian qualities. Christians are a forgiving people. The attitudes of Christians toward their fellow man should be one of forgiving.

Christians who have a forgiving spirit will pray for their fellowman and seek reconciliation when his brother or sister offends them.

The Ability to Forgive and Forget is One of the Fundamental Teachings of the Gospel of Jesus Christ

---

THOU SHALT NOT GOSSIP

Leviticus19: 16 Thou shalt not go up and down as a talebearer among thy people: (KJV)

One of the greatest challenges that face the contemporary Church Community is to overcome the desire to participate in aimless gossip, which leads to falsehoods and character assassination. Christians must always be aware that it is more blessed to talk to others for helping them than to talk about others for harming them.

Gossip and false accusations within the Christian Community is a negative force, which has robbed many otherwise loving Christians of an effective witness within the Church and Community. Rumors spread by Christian brothers and sisters have caused a lot of pain within the Body of Christ. Aimless character assassination serves no spiritual purpose within the Kingdom of God.

The person who participates in negative gossip is on a path of destruction, for when one verbally tears down his brother or sister, they rebel against Christian values and ethics. Gossip is defined as a groundless rumor, or idle chatter. The Bible gives a stern warning against gossip. Psalms

50:20 says: "Thou sittest and speakest against thy brother; thou slanderest thine own mother's son." (KJV)

Aimless gossip has a way of returning to the participant. For many times the person who participates in gossip becomes the object of gossip himself. Building up one 's brother or sister through prayer and fellowship is much more beneficial than tearing them down through gossip and false rumors. The Bible says in Romans 14:10-12: "But why dost thou judge thy brother? or why dost thou set at nought thy brother? for we shall all stand before the judgment seat of Christ... For it is written, As I live, saith the Lord, every knee shall bow to me, and every tongue shall confess to God" ...Every person will give an account of himself to God therefore; speak well of your brother for it is the Christian way.

Groundless Gossip Has Caused a Lot of Pain Within the Christian Family. It Has No Place in Christian Fellowship

---

The Church

CHURCH

Hebrews 12: 23 To the general assembly and church of the
firstborn, which are written in heaven, and to God the Judge
of all, and to the spirits of just men made perfect. (KJV)

In the New Testament the word "Church" is translated from the Greek term ecclesia which refers to an assembly of people and not a building.[1]

Acts 20: 7-8 reads:

> And upon the first day of the week, when the disciples came together to break bread, Paul preached unto them, ready to depart on the morrow; and continued his speech until midnight...And there were many lights in the upper chamber, where they were gathered together." (KJV)

The true Church is found in the heart of the believer. Those who have confessed with their mouth and believed in their heart that Jesus Christ is their Lord and Savior compose the Body of Christ, which is the Church.

1 Corinthians 12:13 reads:

> For by one Spirit are we all baptized into one body, whether we be Jews or Gentiles, whether we be bond or free; and have been all made to drink into one Spirit. (KJV)

Each church member brings his or her own individual talents and gifts.

I Corinthians 12:28 reads:

> "And God hath set some in the Church, first apostles, secondarily prophets, thirdly teachers, after that miracles, then gifts of healings, helps, governments, diversities of tongues." (KJV)

Jesus Christ divinely established the Church. Matthew 16:18 reads

> "And I say also unto thee, That thou art Peter, and upon this rock I will build my Church; and the gates of hell shall not prevail against it." (KJV)

Ephesians 2:19-20 says:

> "Now therefore ye are no more strangers and foreigners, but fellow citizens with the saints and of the household of God; And are built upon the foundation of the apostles and prophets, Jesus Christ himself the chief corner stone;" (KJV)

Jesus Christ is the foundation of the Church. Those who join the Church should totally submit to the will of Jesus.

Colossians 1:17-20 reads:

> And he is before all things, and by him all things consist...And he is the head of the body, the church: who is the beginning, the firstborn from the dead; that in all things he might have the preeminence...For it pleased the Father that in him should all fullness dwell; And having made peace through the blood of his cross, by him to reconcile all things unto himself; by him, I say, whether they be things in earth or things in heaven." (KJV)

Jesus Christ loved the Church and he gave himself for it. The Church is obligated to share the good news of the gospel that Jesus was crucified on the cross, but arose the third day in triumph over death and the grave, and that he grants salvation to lost men and women when they confess with their mouths and believe in their hearts that Jesus is Lord and Savior.

I Corinthians 15:55-57 reads:

> "O death, where is thy sting? O grave, where is thy victory? The sting of death is sin: and the strength of sin is the law...but thanks be to God, which giveth us the victory through our Lord Jesus Christ." (KJV

> Victory over death and the grave is discussed in the above passage of scripture. Salvation in Jesus Christ is discussed in Acts 2:38: "Then Peter said unto them, Repent, and be baptized every one of you in the name of Jesus Christ for the remission of sins, and ye shall receive the gift of the Holy Ghost." (KJV)

The true Church is involved in the ministry of counseling, visitation, addressing human needs, such as hunger and poverty and sharing the good news of the Gospel. Church members are reminded to examine themselves to make sure that they are making the best use of their talents and gifts.

Being listed on the Church roll does not satisfy all the requirements to share in the fullness of the Kingdom of God. Personal involvement in ministry is one of the keys which opens the door to joy in the Kingdom. Jesus was personally involved in the lives of people outside of the Church Establishment. Believers should follow his example of ministry. Christians are the hands and feet of God and every believer will give an account of their earthly stewardship on the Day of Judgment.

Be a Friend to the Lonely and the Disenchanted

Jesus spent considerable time with people who had no status or position, they were the lonely and disenchanted children who had no hope and widows who had no families and men and women who had questionable character. The love of Jesus knew no bounds. He placed his hands on the runny soars of social outcasts who were lepers healing and giving them comfort.

Others were demon-possessed people who reached out for deliverance from a life of torment. The blind, the deaf and the lame who looked for hope and deliverance were also his constituents. The Contemporary Church need to follow the example of Jesus by showing love and compassion to the lonely and disenchanted.

The Mission of the Church

Jesus says in Matthew 28: 19 "Go ye therefore, and teach all nations, baptizing them in the name of the Father, and of the Son, and of the Holy Ghost:"

All believers are called to share the good news of the Jesus Christ. Evangelism is not just the responsibility of the pastor, Sunday school teachers, deacons or trustees; the entire Church membership is responsible for evangelizing.

Philippians 2: 10-12 says " That at the name of Jesus every knee should bow, of *things* in heaven, and *things* in earth, and things under the earth; __11__ And *that* every tongue should confess that Jesus Christ *is* Lord, to the glory of God the Father. All believers have a job to perform in the Kingdom of God.

Evangelism Methods

Believers can promote evangelism through their financial giving.

Malachi 3: [8] Will a man rob God? Yet ye have robbed me. But ye say, wherein have we robbed thee? In tithes and offerings. [9] Ye are cursed with a curse: for ye have robbed me, even this whole nation.[10] Bring ye all the tithes into the storehouse, that there may be meat in mine house, and prove me now herewith, saith the Lord of hosts, if I will not open you the windows of heaven, and pour you out a blessing, that there shall not be room enough to receive it.

Those who contribute to Home and Foreign missions and give their tithes and offerings to the local church aid in the evangelism effort.

Believers can evangelize through the Power of Prayer and through an expression of Love and Compassion

Jesus had compassion for the lost and sinners.

Luke 15 [4] "What man of you, having a hundred sheep, if he loses one of them, does not leave the ninety-nine in the wilderness, and go after the one which is lost until he finds it? [5] And when he has found *it*, he lays *it* on his shoulders, rejoicing. [6] And when he comes home, he calls together *his* friends and neighbors, saying to them, 'Rejoice with me, for I have found my sheep which was lost!' [7] I say to you that likewise there will be more joy in heaven over one sinner who repents than over ninety-nine just persons who need no repentance.

Evangelize through your personal behavior; a believer's lifestyle impacts the lives of non-believers

Matthew 5 [16] Let your light so shine before men, that they may see your good works and glorify your Father in heaven.

Evangelize through distributing salvation materials and tracks

Paul evangelized through the written and the preached word. Paul wrote 14 of the 27 books of the New Testament.

2 Timothy 3:16

> [16] All Scripture *is* given by inspiration of God, and *is* profitable for doctrine, for reproof, for correction, for instruction in righteousness.

Evangelize through teaching the word

God commands his followers to teach his word.

Deuteronomy 6 [4] "Hear, O Israel: The LORD our God, the LORD is one![a] [5] You shall love the LORD your God with all your heart, with all your soul, and with all your strength. [6] "And these words which I command you today shall be in your heart. [7] You shall teach them diligently to your children and shall talk of them when you sit in your house, when you walk by the way, when you lie down, and when you rise. [8] You shall bind them as a sign on your hand, and they shall be as frontlets between your eyes.

Evangelize through preaching the Word

Preaching the Word is the most common method of evangelism most preachers end with an invitation to discipleship.

1 Chronicles 16:23-24

> [23] Sing unto the LORD, all the earth; shew forth from day to day his salvation.
> [24] Declare his glory among the heathen; his marvelous works among all nations.

Evangelize through Church revivals

Church sponsored evangelism and revival services are some of the most popular ways to share the good news of Jesus Christ.

Evangelize through evangelism workshops and seminars

Evangelism workshops and seminars is also an effective way of sharing the good news of Jesus Christ.

Evangelize through personal words of witness

All believers should know how to witness to the unsaved and the lost.

All believers are called to evangelize

Matthew 28: 18-20 says [18] And Jesus came and spake unto them, saying, all power is given unto me in heaven and in earth.[19] Go ye therefore, and teach all nations, baptizing them in the name of the Father, and of the Son, and of the Holy Ghost:[20] Teaching them to observe all things whatsoever I have commanded you: and, lo, I am with you always, even unto the end of the world. Amen.

Believers must send positive signals to those around them

When others see the Fruit of the Spirit in a
believer's life evangelism is enhanced.

The secondary mission of the Church

- Promote or institute a strong Christian education program
- Train believers to be effective ambassadors for Jesus Christ
- Develop strong Christian character within the church membership
- Promote Sunday school, Church training, Bible study and Prayer meetings
- Address the spiritual needs of different age groups such as children, youth, adults, seniors, married couples and singles
- Minister to the elderly and the less fortunate
- Minister to those who are in rest homes, prisons, hospitals, the sick and shut-in and the less fortunate
- Sponsor Christian education workshops and seminars
- Develop programs that strengthen the family
- Encourage families to remain focused on a Christian lifestyle
- Develop strategies to combat an entertainment media complex that has produced programs which are not youth and family friendly
- Avoid a lifestyle of cheating. lying, cussing, drinking, smoking, sex outside of marriage and adultery
- Support parents in teaching children and youth to respect   authority
- Develop youth self-esteem programs
- Teach youth about their heritage
- Encourage youth to reach their full spiritual and academic potential

How to achieve the Mission of the Church?

- Be born again; the blind cannot lead the blind
- Pray for the guidance of the Holy Spirit
- Rely on prayer

- Seek godly counsel
- Walk in the Spirit avoid walking in the Flesh
- Work together in a spirit of love and unity

Christian Mission Advice

- Churches are encouraged to have specific time slots for Church training and Christian education programming. It could be one or two Sunday evening time slots.
- Each Church has a personality. Day and time slots of programs can be adjusted to address the needs of the church.
- Christian education workers should work with the pastor to assign a specific time slot for Christian education training.
- Church leaders should do everything in their power to make sure that they are taking advantage of positive Christian resources that are available to help their church to promote and achieve effective Christian missions.
- The Word of God holds the key to promoting effective Christian missions.
- Each person is encouraged to read and study the Word of God and pray for an understanding to address the accountability for effective Christian missions.

Church Leadership

Definition of Christian Leadership

Christian Leadership is the ability to motivate others to achieve the stated goals and objectives of the Teachings of Christ.

Leadership Skills are divided into three Categories

A. **Diagnostic Skills**

   The ability to identify a problem and find a solution

B. **Perceptual Skills**

   - the ability to communicate and motivate with words
   - the ability to listen without interruption

C. **Organizational Skills**

   - Teamwork Skills
   - Teambuilding Skills
   - Negotiation Skills
   - Delegation Skills
   - Motivation Skills
   - Coaching Skills
   - Counseling Skills

Perquisites for Christian Leadership

- Salvation (A leader must be saved; the blind cannot lead the blind.)
- Constant prayer is essential.
- A sense of dedication (Christian leaders must have a sense of purpose and have the will to achieve stated goals and objectives.)
- An unselfish Spirit of Love (Christian leaders must possess a sense of love for God and their fellow man.)
- A Spirit of Service and Humility (Christians leaders must be willing to work toward improving the welfare of others.)
- A Spiritual Vision (Christian leaders must possess a hunger for righteousness and a vision to up build the kingdom of God.)
- Written Goals and Objectives (Clearly defined goals and objectives are essential to Christian Leadership.)
- An Action Plan (Christian Leaders must have an effective Action Plan.)

Ingredients of an effective Action Plan

- Assemble a team of capable associates to help with planning and decision making.
- Thoroughly explain your action plan to make sure that everyone is on board.
- Place the right people in the right positions.
- Communicate with your associates on a regular basis; it may mean bi weekly or monthly meetings.
- Evaluate the progress of stated goals and objectives on a regular basis and make changes when necessary.
- Make sure that you have materials and financial resources.
- Activate your action plan at the appropriate time.

Obstacles to Christian Leadership

- Self-Serving Pride
- Immorality (a sinful lifestyle)
- Greed (leadership abuse of power)
- Low Mental and Physical Energy
- The inability to accept criticism
- Failure to delegate duties and responsibilities
- Failure to grow Spiritually

- Family Neglect
- Incompetent Administrative Skills
- Failure to Spend Sufficient Time in Preparation
- Failure to Spend Sufficient Time in Bible Study and Prayer

Formula for Strong Christian Leadership

- have an unobstructed vision and a sense of purpose and direction (the kind of vision and sense of purpose that Dr. Martin Luther King and Dr. Billy Graham had
- have clearly defined goals and specific objectives
- possess a genuine belief that Christian Leadership is needed
- have the same faith that Sarah and Abraham had when they sojourned into a distant land
- possess a burning desire to make a difference in the lives of others, the same kind of desire that the Apostle Paul had when he established churches through Asia Minor

Effective Christian Leadership Process

- A Sense of Purpose
- A Willingness to Learn
- A Dedication to God
- A Realistic Attitude
- Genuine Character
- Openness to innovative ideas

Character matters because the public tends to mimic the behavior of their leaders. Christian leaders are encouraged to set positive examples through their words and deeds. All church leaders have a responsibility to be up right Christian citizens.

Godly Leadership Profile (Abraham)

God spoke to Abraham and told him to leave his hometown and go into a strange land (Genesis 11: 31-32)

- Abraham obeyed God by leaving his home (Acts 7: 2-4)
- Abraham praised God by building a worship altar to the Lord and called upon his name (Genesis 12:7-9)

- Worship and Praise was very important to Abraham therefore worship and praise should be important to us
- Abraham experienced family problems (his son Ishmael and his bond maiden Hagar were cast out of his home) Christian leaders will experience trials and tribulations

In the Christian Life there is usually, the break through, the disappointment and then the miracle. The break through comes when a believer is called to a position of Christian leadership; the disappointment comes when a servant of God is criticized for using his or her gifts to help build the Kingdom of God. The miracles come when a believer keeps the faith during challenging times. There is a reward when Christian Leaders continue to obey God through trials, tribulations and criticism.

- Abraham thrived through failure and adversity. He did not allow his shortcomings to destroy his goals and objectives.
- Abraham demonstrated his faith. He was willing to sacrifice his son Isaac because he believed that God would make a way out of no way. (Genesis 22: 16-18)
- God blessed the obedience of Abraham. (Genesis 22: 16-18)

Developing Leadership Skills

- Stay focused on the primary goal of your organization
- Assemble a team of capable persons, those who think for themselves who may not agree with you all the time
- Seek help from others who have different skills and abilities
- Get feedback from those who observe you from a unique perspective
- Know your strengths and weaknesses and seek help when you need it
- Don't be afraid of failure

The Five C's of leadership

Character

People are looking for honest, sincere leaders.

Caring

People are inspired by leaders who are compassionate and truly care.

Commitment

True leaders stay the course in good and tough times.

Confidence

Leaders who know how to succeed and have the will to succeed inspire confidence.

Communication

Great leaders can convince others to receive and believe in a vision.

Seven Keys to effective Leadership

- don't use your influence until you get some
- keep your promises
- be optimistic believe success can be achieved
- seek advice from those who can help you succeed
- listen to constructive criticism
- praise the small steps that other people make
- have a sense of caring and concern

Effective leaders solve problems

- write the problem on paper
- identity the reasons the problem exists
- state workable solutions
- brain storm and decide on the best solution
- develop a plan to solve the problem
- implement the plan

Leadership qualities of Dr. Martin Luther and Dr. Billy Graham

- had no identity problem they knew who they were
- were aware of their strengths and weaknesses
- knew about their background and heritage

- were inspired by the Holy Spirit
- had compassion for the disadvantage
- were men of faith they knew the source of their strength
- were positive persons who believed in the potential for positive relationships among persons of all races and cultures
- exhibited courage in the face of danger
- believed in thorough preparation
- had an unobstructed vision, they knew what they wanted to achieve
- possessed superior communication skills
- refused to compromise their ideas, they spoke boldly on the issues regardless of the audience or the occasion
- were confident that positive change could occur

What made Sister Rosa Parks a strong Leader?

- strong convictions and a deep sense of personal pride in the cause of civil rights
- firm faith in the face of danger
- a willing to sacrifice herself for a greater cause
- had a sense of history
- realized the importance of the moment
- stayed the course in good times and tough times
- consistent positive character over an extended period
- had a strong faith and a sense of purpose
- refused to be a second-class citizen
- had a great deal of self-respect

Christian Leaders need to be aware of Contemporary Leadership Issues

- Aids and Sexual disease crises
- Changing weather patterns, global warming issues
- Growing energy concerns
- Sexual Predators
- Confidential and privacy issues
- An increased aging population
- A constant war cycle and growing unrest
- An increased drug and crime wave

- Rising single families and divorce rates
- An aggressive Gay Rights movement
- Low performing schools
- Rebellion against authority and the Christian Church
- An open challenge to marriage and the family
- Growing racial tension and concerns

Church Administration

What is Church Administration?

Effective Church administration is a spiritual management plan that maximizes the following church resources:

- spiritual
- people
- financial
- facility
- material
- equipment

The pastor is the primary visible head of the church and is the chief administrator or works closely the official Church administrators

Who initiates effective Church administration?

Those who have the proper gifts or training and are led by the Holy Spirit initiates effective Church administration.

Ways to maintain effective church administration?

- Communicate
- Plan
- Pray
- Research

- Spend financial resources when necessary
- Seek information from informed sources

Effective Church Administrators

- are led by the Holy Spirit
- work with the pastor, the trustees, the financial sectary and others who deal with the finances of the church to find ways to more efficiently manage the monies of the church
- research ways to more efficiently perform their duties
- study the Word of God and believe in the power prayer
- implement the directives, the teachings or the commands of our Lord and Savior Jesus Christ
- are required to know the purpose and the mission of the church, (which is to share the good news of the gospel with all men, women, boys and girls)
- highlights the Plan of Salvation, the Power of Prayer and the Guidance of the Holy Ghost
- promotes discipleship training which leads to Christian maturity
- believes in the power of Prayer and obeys the Word of God
- live Christian lives and give financial and spiritual support to the church
- are visionaries who understand the importance of planning for the future
- are born again Christians who know how to build and maintain positive relationships.
- knows how to delegate responsibility
- makes sure that the church membership is informed about major church projects that involves finances

Church Stewardship Accountability

Defining Christian Accountability

Christian Accountability is an obligation and the responsibility to use God given Spiritual and Material resources to promote the Teachings of Jesus Christ.

Defining Christian Stewardship

Christian stewardship is a spiritual management system that requires a Christian steward or believer to do everything in their power to maximize the spiritual and the material resources of the church for achieving the work of the Kingdom of God in an efficient, effective and spiritual way.

Shared Information on Christian stewardship

- A Christian steward is one who has been granted the responsibility of managing the spiritual gifts, the material gifts or the God given talents of the Heavenly Father.
- A Christian steward does not have full possession of spiritual gifts, talents or materials possessions. Everything belongs to God. Psalms **24:1 says the earth is the Lord's and the fullness thereof; the world and they that dwell in it.** God is the sole owner of all spiritual gifts, talents and material possessions.
- If a Christian steward does not follow the instructions or the directions of the Heavenly Father; his or her spiritual gifts can be taken away and given to another who will follow the Father's will. A Christian steward serves at the discretion of the Father who is in Heaven.
- A steward is accountable and responsible for the proper use of their spiritual gifts or talents whether they be spiritual or material in nature.
- Spiritual and material blessings are received when we give of our tithes and offerings. Malachi 3: 10 says Bring ye all the tithes into the storehouse, that there may be meat in mine house, and prove me now herewith, saith the LORD of hosts, if I will not open you the windows of heaven, and pour you out a blessing, that there shall not be room enough to receive it.
- There is a blessing when we fellow the teachings of the Scripture but there are consequences when a believer fails to activate their God given gifts or talents or when they use them to abuse or mistreat their fellowman.
- When it is said and done Christian stewards are required to use their spiritual gifts, talents, time and financial and material resources for the up building of the Kingdom of God.
- Based on the scripture every Christian steward will give and account of their stewardship for Romans 14: 11-12 says for it is written, As I live, saith the Lord, every knee shall bow to me, and every tongue shall confess to God. 12   So then every one of us shall give account of himself to God.

The Whole Duty of Man

Ecclesiastes 12: 13-14 says

> [13] Let us hear the conclusion of the whole matter: Fear God and keep his commandments: for this *is* the whole *duty* of man. [14] For God shall bring every work into judgment, with every secret thing, whether *it be* good, or whether *it be* evil.

Church Music

Worship with Church Music

Music played a prominent role in the lives of ancient people. It was used in war, in magic, in worship, in work and in various sorts of social activities such as parties, banquets and parades.[1] David was a talented composer and musician as was evident in the composition of the 144 Psalms. The Psalms gives a revealing insight of David's love for God through poetry and song.

Music appeals to that which is beautiful and ecstatic man. Music is a universal language, which cuts across all cultures and social economic backgrounds.

Music is thought to have therapeutic qualities, which helps in the psychological healing of certain persons. David played the harp for Saul to ward off what was said to be the torment of an evil spirit.

1 Samuel 16:15-16 reads:

> "And Saul's servants said unto him, Behold now, an evil spirit from God troubleth thee...Let our Lord now command thy servants, which are before thee, to seek out a man, who is a cunning player on an harp: and it shall come to pass, when the evil spirit from God is upon thee, that he shall play with his hand, and thou shalt be well." (KJV

GENERAL CATEGORIES OF CHURCH MUSIC

There is a Variety of Church Music

There are various categories of church music and each category has unique qualities and characteristics. The common ground of all church music should be that it is sung to the glory of God, written in dedication to the worship of Jesus Christ, or composed in the praise of his personal attributes such as love, peace or joy. The glory and the majesty of the Savior should be manifested in all church music.

CATEGORIES:

Hymns: A hymn is a song or ode in praise, adoration or supplication of God.[2] Some of the great hymn writers were Isaac Watts (1674-1748) "Joy to the World" 1719; Charles Wesley (1703-1791) A Charge to Keep I Have" 1762; John Newton (1725-1807) Amazing Grace! How Sweet the Sound" 1792.

These great composers wrote hundreds of hymns during their long productive lives. Church worship services have been immensely enriched because of the contributions of great hymn writers who felt inspired by God to write songs, which have given us hope through the "Joy" of heavenly music.

Anthem: An anthem is a piece of choral music sung in recognition of a national theme.[3] "The Star-Spangled Banner" written by Francis Scott Key is the American National Anthem, and "Lift Every Voice and Sing" written by James Weldon Johnson is the National Black Hymn. These are examples of anthems which are appropriate to sing at designated times during the worship service.

Spirituals: A Spiritual is a religious song asserting a strong simple faith sung originally by black slaves in the South.[4] Spirituals are rooted in the Black Christian experience. The black slaves sung from the depths of their hearts as they toiled in the cotton fields of the South. They sang a song of joy and pain mixed in the same lyrics.

Some Familiar Spirituals Are:

- "Roll, Jordan Roll"
- "Go Down Moses"
- "O What A Beautiful City"
- "Wade in The Water"
- "Joshua Fought the Battle of Jericho
- "Swing Low"
- "There's No Hiding Place Down Here"

Gospel Music: Joseph C. Pyles in his article Music in the Black Church says, "Gospels are modern jazz improvisations of spirituals and hymns.[5] Gospel songs appeal to the emotions of persons and the songs have very expressive lyrics.

America has seen the rise of African American Gospel and the emergence of Southern Country Gospel. These are two very different forms of gospel, which has evolved over the years based on the cultural differences of the two groups.

It is obvious that Southern Country Gospel and African American Gospel are distinctly different. But, they share a common characteristic in that they are both emotionally charged forms of music that appeals to the "joy" of life which should be in the hearts of every Christian.

The word "gospel" originates from the old Anglo-Saxon word "GodSpell," meaning God Story or Narrative of God.[6] Ideally the lyrics of a gospel song should be dedicated to the praise of Jesus Christ or to some characteristics or attribute of Jesus such as love, joy, peace or victory.

Music Ministry

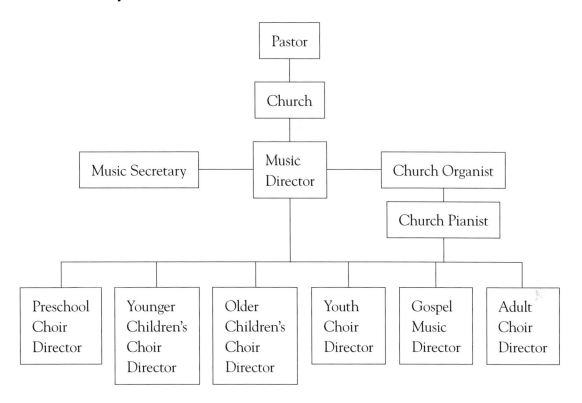

Setting personal ambitions aside and singing for the glory of God is a very noble choir objective. When choir members become preoccupied with their personal talents and project their talents as a badge of superiority, they run the risk of losing sight of the fact that their talents were given to them by God and that they could lose their talents through abuse or misuse.

When choir members pray and read the Word of God and focus their attention upon the teachings of Jesus Christ, there is less time for gossip, confusion and misunderstandings. The choir serves a noble function. It is one of the most visible organizations within the Church. Choir members, like all born again Christians, should project a spirit of love and peace, and set a good example for youth and the Church.

HYMNAL RESOURCE VALUE

The Church members who take the time to review the Church hymnal do a great service because the hymnal is a great music resource.

> General Hymnal Outline:
> Table of Contents
> Church Covenant
> Hymns page by page
> Appendix
> - Responsive Reading:
> - Call of Worship
> - Benediction
> - Articles of Faith
> - Topical Index for Hymns
> - Index of First Lines and Titles

Information in the Baptist Church hymnals is a valuable resource.

Some churches are abandoning Church musical traditions such as Hymns. Contemporary Church Music has replaced most of the Great Hymns. There are certain traditions that churches should to hold on to. Singing Church Hymns is one of them. Highlighting Traditional and Contemporary Church Music can add to the spiritual integrity of the worship service. Our fore parents have given much to the Church by way of preaching, teaching and music. Let's honor them by maintaining some their traditions.

The Contemporary Church will be blessed if it honors its spiritual roots. Ships that are far away from the shore have a greater chance to sink than those close to the shore. The old landmarks have a place in the Contemporary Church for they remind us where we have come from. Believers who know where they come from or know about their roots are in a better position to achieve the goals of Christian Ministry. The Contemporary Church could benefit by honoring some of the Traditional Church Landmarks that have withstood the test of time.

Giving and Stewardship to God

Tithing Diagram

Salary	Tithe
$10.00	$1.00
$20.00	$2.00
$30.00	$3.00
$60.00	$6.00
$100.00	$10.00
$200.00	$20.00
$350.00	$35.00
$500.00	$50.00
$750.00	$75.00
$1000.00	$100.00
$2000.00	$200.00
$3000.00	$300.00

GIVING AND STEWARDSHIP TO GOD

Stewardship is the Key to Financial Success

A steward is one who is trusted with something that belongs to someone else.[1] The air we breathe, the food we eat, the water we drink, the earth we walk on belongs to God. He is the sole owner of the world. He created the heavens, the earth, the moon, the stars and every living thing that creeps upon the earth.

By God's ownership of the world, we own nothing but have been trusted with certain gifts to share with others[2]. The money we have, the homes we live in, the cars we drive, the clothes we wear and even the children we are blessed with belong to God.

Man cannot exist aside from God because he is the source of health and strength. When a person accepts the pre-eminence of God in his or her life, they will cheerfully give of their money and time to the Church.

Job accepted the pre-eminence of God in his life. He said, "the Lord giveth and the Lord taketh away, blessed is the name of the Lord." Job was a steward. He had been trusted with many resources from God: cattle, land, a family, excellent health and strength.

One day God permitted Satan to take these possessions away. But, Job remained faithful and patient through trials and tribulations. Job knew the source of his blessings were the almighty and the all wise God. He said he was naked when he came into the world and he would be naked when going out of the world. He knew that God was the source of his blessings and that he was not the sole owner of anything.

Job served the Lord in the best of times and in the worst of times. A steward is to serve God unconditionally. He is to never stop serving God, because God is the source of all being. We learn from the story of Job that all his resources were restored and increased over what he originally had because he remained steadfast in the rains and storms of life.

SCRIPTURE ON STEWARDSHIP

God expects us to be good Stewards of His resources

Matthew 21:33-41

Jesus tells the parable of the husbandman. There was a housekeeper who planted a vineyard and went off into a far country and left the vineyard in the care of a husbandman. When time to harvest the fruit drew near, he sent a servant to the husbandman that he would receive some of the fruit. The husbandman beat the servant and killed another and stoned another. The householder sent more servants, but the same thing happened. Then he sent his beloved son and the husbandman caught him and slew him.

The parable tells the story of an unrighteous steward who abused the substance of his master. When he slew the master's beloved son, the master took away his resources and gave them to others who were more responsible and accountable. The Lord expects us to be good stewards of the resources he has blessed us with.

1 Corinthians 4:1-2

1. Let a man so account of us, as of the ministers of Christ, and stewards of the mysteries of God.
2. Moreover it is required in stewards, that a man be found faithful."

A Tithing Church is Generally a Blessed Church

Paul says in the preceding scripture that a steward should be faithful. He should trust the Lord and believe that the Lord will bless him. The Bible teaches that Christian stewardship will be rewarded.

TITHING

Malachi 3:10 says:

> "Bring ye all the tithes into the storehouse, that there may be meat in mine house, and prove me now here with, saith the Lord of hosts, if I will not open you the windows of heaven, and pour you out a blessing, that there shall not be room enough to receive it. (KJV)

The wisdom of sharing one's resources and time is deeply rooted in the teachings of Jesus Christ.

Matthew 10:42 says:

> "And whosoever shall give to drink unto one of these little ones a cup of cold water only in the name of a disciple, verily I say unto you, he shall in no wise lose his reward." (KJV)

Genesis 14:20 says:

> "And blessed be the most high God, which hath delivered thine enemies into thy hand. And he gave him tithes of all." (KJV) This scripture refers to the tithe; Abraham gave to Melchizedek, King of Salem who symbolized the king of peace and righteousness.

Hebrews 7:1-2 says:

> For this Melchizedek, king of Salem, priest of the Most High God, who met Abraham returning from the slaughter of the kings and blessed him, [2]to whom also Abraham gave a tenth part of all, first being translated "king of righteousness," and after that also king of Salem which is "King of peace," KJV)

This passage of scripture says that when Abraham paid tithes to Melchizedek, (he paid it to an eternal order of righteousness and justice.) Abraham received many blessings because of his benevolence and obedience. In Genesis 22:17 we get a picture of Abraham's blessings after he obediently offered his son Isaac as a sacrifice.

> "That in blessing I will bless thee, and in multiplying I will multiply thy seed as
> the stars of the heaven, and as the sand which is upon the sea shore; and thy
> seed shall possess the gate of his enemies;" (KJV)

The blessings of God are a consistent theme when there is mention of a person giving or being obedient to the word of God.

Leviticus 27:30 says:

> "And all the tithe of the land, whether of the seed of the land, or of the fruit of
> the tree, is the Lord's: it is holy unto the Lord." (KJV)

The writer of Leviticus reminds us that the earth is the Lord's and the fullness there of. All the resources we possess come from God. When we tithe we acknowledge the ownership of God and the greatness of his glory. Our tithes aid in the sharing and the spreading of his eternal blessings. The church, which tithes, is obedient to the teachings of the scripture.

The scripture says that the Lord spoke unto Moses as recorded in Numbers 18:26:

> Thus speak unto the Levites, and say unto them, When ye take of the children
> of Israel the tithes which I have given you from them for your inheritance, then
> ye shall offer up an heave offering of it for the Lord, even a tenth part of the
> tithe." (KJV)

We are reminded in Numbers that in the day of Moses, the Priest and the Levites who were attendants in the temple were dependent upon the giving of the people. We are also reminded that when a priest or Levite received their pay, they owed a tithe to the Lord. No believer is totally exempt from the tithe. Those who fail to tithe will miss out on a blessing.

Deuteronomy 14:28 says:"

> At the end of three years thou shalt bring forth all the tithe of thine increase
> the same year, and shalt lay it up within thy gates:" (KJV)

In the Old Testament, the children of Israel were required to tithe by law every third and sixth year. The Levites of the priestly order administered the tithes and laid them at the gates to feed the stranger, the fatherless and the widows. The relief of human suffering has been a primary purpose for the giving of tithes and offerings.

Matthew 23:23 says:

> "Woe unto you, Scribes and Pharisees, hypocrites! for ye pay tithe of mint and anise and cummin, and have omitted the weightier matters of the law, judgment, mercy and faith: these ought ye to have done, and not to leave the other undone." (KJV)

The Pharisees were some of the most self-righteous people who ever lived. They were students of the law. They performed various functions that appeared to be right. They paid their tithes but did not pay them in the right spirit because they showed very little mercy and love toward those who were not as zealous in keeping the law as they did. Tithe in the spirit of love and peace for it is a key to spiritual and financial blessing.

Stewardship is one of the most prominent messages in the Scripture. The first man Adam was given the responsibility of maintaining and supervising all the activities in the Garden of Eden. Everything in the garden was a gift from God. The trees, food, shelter, beauty, air, and animals were a part of the garden because God allowed it to be so. Man's entire existences is due to the creative power of God.

Man does not own anything, everything belongs to God. Stewardship requires that we maintain and take care of everything that God has given to us. The Contemporary Church has been given a fantastic opportunity to succeed. There are boundless people and material resources; it up to the pastor and the Church leadership to take advantage of the available resources. When it is all said and done man will give an account of his stewardship of God's resources. All churches are encouraged to be good stewards of the gifts that God has given.

The Role of the Deacon and the Deaconess

DEACON

Called to Help Build the Kingdom of God
Through Christian Character and Service

The word deacon is derived from the Greek noun diakonos servant, minister or attendant.[1] Traditionally the first deacons were called to aid the disciples in the distribution of goods to the Greek widows in Jerusalem. However, the book of Acts does not refer to them as deacons.

Acts 6:3 says the seven men would be of honest report, full of the Holy Ghost and wisdom. The appointing of the seven servants allowed the disciples to continuously pray and preach the good news of the gospel.

Acts 6:5 (KJV) names the following men as the seven servants (which we refer to as deacons in the contemporary church)

- Stephen was a man of faith and full of the Holy Ghost
- Philip
- Prochorus
- Nicanor
- Timon
- Parmenas
- Nicolas, a proselyte in Antioch

The Primary Role of the Deacon

Unyielding Christian Service

According to Acts 6:1-6 (KJV) the deacon was called to serve. He was not called to a position of celebrated authority, for his honor and prestige came through his service to the church. Many times, a deacon's sacrifice, challenging work and dedication may go unnoticed, but they will receive their just reward because God never forgets an obedient servant.

Supplemental Duties of the Deacon

- Visit the sick and shut-in
- Assist in the worship in the absence of the pastor
- Pray and care the welfare of the church membership
- Open and lock church building before and after church meetings
- Assist in worship and baptismal service
- Prepare and fill the baptismal pool
- Listen to needs of the congregation
- Inform pastor of critical church needs and the concerns of the congregation
- Give spiritual support to the pastor and church during worship service
- Assist in the communion observance, placing communion table, praying for the bread and wine, distributing bread and wine, collecting bread and wine containers
- Assist during the right hand of fellowship
- Encourage members to fully participate in church activities
- Promote harmony and good will among the membership
- When requested, assist the pastor in the worship services
- Pray for the success of the church program
- Assist in the collection of tithes and offerings
- Should be a faithful steward in the giving of his time and finances to the church program
- Assist the church with tithes and offering

Relationship to the Pastor

A Loyal Friend and a Dedicated Servant of the Lord

The deacon is a church appointed assistant to the pastor. The pastor is placed over the church by both the appointment of God and by the free and voluntary act of the church itself. *(Hiscox)[2]

The deacon who honors the biblical notion that the pastorship is the highest earthly position in the Church will likely be an ally to the pastor rather than a rival for the leadership of the church.

The Church is a team and each member on the team has a specific role. The deacon who is a team player is a great aid to the pastor in helping him to nurture and build the kingdom of God.

Ordination of the Deacons

A Loyal Church Member and Servant

According to Acts 6:6 the apostles prayed and laid hands on the seven as a sign of ordination. Being appointed as a deacon is serious business. Ordination in the church generally denotes sacredness. The ordained servant has the blessings of the church and pastor.

The deacon has a grave responsibility for he is to represent the church in accordance to the teachings of Jesus Christ. There should be no conflict in his words and deeds. The deacon's life should be one of inspiration to the saved as well as the unsaved.

QUALIFICATIONS

A Sincere Love for the Lord and a Sense of Dedication to the Mission of the Church

---

The qualifications of a deacon are found in I Timothy 3:8-13 and in Acts 6:3.

- <u>Grave</u> **(I Timothy 3:8)** One who is serious about spiritual matters and takes pride in the work of the church
- <u>Not Double Tongued</u> **(I Timothy 3:8)** A man of his word, one who is consistent in word and deed
- <u>Not Given to too Much Wine</u> **(I Timothy 3:8)** A good steward of one's money and time, a responsible sensible person who is not overly concerned about temporary pleasures, which last but a short time
- <u>Not Greedy of Filthy Lucre</u> **(I Timothy 3:8)** A man who seeks first the kingdom of God and his righteousness, and knows that material possessions bring no lasting satisfaction
- <u>Faithful with a Pure Conscience</u> **(I Timothy 3:9)** One who is in control of his emotions and does not allow the troubles of this world overwhelm him
- <u>Proved and Tested</u> **(I Timothy 3:10)** A man who has demonstrated Christian maturity in his speech and actions, one who shows courage in the face of trials and tribulations
- <u>Blameless</u> **(I Timothy 3:10)** A man who has a good reputation, who is a law abiding Christian citizen
- <u>Support of Wife</u> **(I Timothy 3:11)** The wife of a deacon should be supportive, not slanderous, sober and faithful
- <u>Husband of One Wife</u> **(I Timothy 3:12)** A faithful devoted husband who loves his wife and is committed to a monogamous marriage
- <u>Family Life</u> **(I Timothy 3:11-12)** A man who support his family and provides for their health and welfare
- <u>Management of Their Children and Their Own Homes Well</u> (I Timothy 3:12) A candidate for the deaconship should show proper love and respect toward his household
- <u>Boldness in the Faith</u> **(I Timothy 3:13)** A man of strong Christian convictions, willing to take a stand because of his love for Christ

- **<u>A Man of Honest Report</u> (Acts 6:3)** A man of strong Christian character in the church as well as the community, must be one who believes in good wholesome Christian principles
- **Full of the Holy Ghost (Acts 6:3)** Led by the Spirit of Jesus Christ
- **Full of Wisdom (Acts 6:3)** Relies on Christian spiritual guidance for knowledge and insight, and seeks the wisdom of God through prayer and the reading of his word
- **Full of Faith (Acts 6:5)** Trust in God rather than material possessions, has the ability to look beyond trials and tribulations to a brighter day

THE DEACONSHIP

United in Christian Service

The collective number of deacons in a specific church composes the deaconship. The presiding deacon is usually elected by the pastor and is usually called the chairman or the senior deacon. Leadership ability or seniority are usually the factors which determine who is elected as chairman or senior deacon.

The Number of Deacons

Many churches maintain the tradition of selecting seven deacons, but a more recent trend has been to select as many deacons as needed to perform the proper task in the church. For example: a church with a membership of 3,000 would probably need more deacons than a church, which has a membership of less than 2,000. A good ratio may be one deacon for every 30 members. The church membership and the pastor are the final authority in deciding how many deacons are needed in their congregations. Guidelines in determining the number of deacons should be recorded in the church's by-laws.

SELECTION PROCESS

Pray for the Guidance of the Holy Spirit
in Selecting Deacon Candidates

The pastor, church members or other deacons usually recommend deaconship candidates. The candidate is usually observed over an extended period.

The pastor and representatives of the deaconship interview recommended candidates who meet the biblical qualifications found in the 6th chapter of Acts. If the pastor and the deaconship agree on the worthiness of the candidate, he is usually presented before the church at the appropriate time set forth in the constitution.

If the candidate is approved through church vote, a date is set for his ordination. Upon his ordination, he receives the right hand of fellowship and becomes a full deacon.

Sample Ordination Service
Prelude
Call to Worship
Hymn
Scripture Reading
The Occasion
- host pastor
- examination board
- church clerk

Charge to the Candidate
Charge to the Church
Hymn
Prayer of Ordination
Hymn
"Laying on of Hands"
Presentation of the Bible
Remarks
Benediction

Junior Deacon Program

An effective way to build church leadership is through a junior deaconship program. The junior deacon is generally a married, young man who meets the **biblical standards** of deaconship but has no slot to serve in.

Preparation is the Best Teacher

Participants who serve in such a program have the opportunity to receive the necessary training to become an effective deacon when the opportunity arises. The program also provides an incentive for participants to become more fully involved in the ministry of the church.

There is no set formula on how the program should be implemented or supervised. Each church in cooperation with the pastor needs to determine the number and the length of time a person serves as a junior deacon.

Maybe the most crucial factor in determining the number and the length of time that a junior deacon should serve is the size of the church enrollment. One suggestion is to have a rotating selection system with each candidate serving a two-year term with a minimum of four participants serving during a given period. It is possible in some small churches to allow junior deacons to serve continuously until a slot opens.

Leadership Training is Essential for Effective Church Programming
---

Training is Necessary for Leadership

Deaconess

Women church servants draw inspiration from Phoebe a servant of the church at Cenchrea a known town east of Corinth. Phoebe was a servant and a church helper. The Greek word for servant is diakonon the English translation is deacon. The female term is deaconess. (Roman 16:1) In many churches deaconess are the wives of deacons. The scripture does not give a detailed list of deaconess qualifications and duties. Most of the duties are traditional in nature.

Suggested Duties

- Prepare Baptismal Role
- Wash and store baptismal clothing
- Assist female baptismal candidates
- Assist the pastor upon request
- Purchase bread and grape juice
- Place Baptismal emblems on the communion table
- Cover baptismal emblems with a white sheet
- Clean and store linen, towel and other baptismal items
- Visit the sick minister and aged minister to new members
- Live an upright Christian life
- Be a regular church attendee
- Support the church with tithes and offering
- Assist minister in addressing female issues

The http://www.plusline.org website was helpful in the writing of this section.

According to the ATS Merriam Webster Dictionary the Greek word for servant is diakonos which in found in Romans 16:1. The word for servant in the Authorized Version is translated as deacon or minister. Phoebe is mentioned as servant in Romans 16:1.

There is very little mention of Phoebe in the bible; her name is only mentioned once in Roman 1: 1-2 where the Apostle Paul commends her as a servant of the church in Cenhreae. Paul asked the Church in Rome to receive her in the Lord in a worthy way and to give her the help she needed to perform her ministry duties. Paul told the Church in Rome that Phoebe had given support to numerous people including himself.

Paul gave Phoebe a great endorsement, he believed that she had several gifts and abilities. Phoebe had earned the respect of the Apostle Paul who was the leading evangelist of his time. If the Apostle Paul honored and celebrated the gifts of Phoebe the Contemporary Church should do likewise.

The Trustee Ministry

The Trustee Ministry

Key Words: Trust, Character, Honesty

Separation of church and state is one of the cornerstones of the Constitution. The desire for religious freedom was the primary reason settlers came to America.

In principle, separation of church and state is the law of the land, but there are state laws relating to religious corporations. These laws require that there be a specific body in the church which holds legal title to the property of the church and is responsible for its financial affairs.[1] The body, which handles such affairs in the church, is usually called trustees. The church trustees have been trusted to maintain and care for the property of the church.

Mature Judgment and a Christian Spirit is Essential in the Character of a Trustee

---

Mature judgement and a Christian spirit are two of the most essential qualities of trustee. Immature or misguided Church financial decisions can cause major problems within the Body of Christ. Some churches have split over poor financial decisions. A mature spiritual trustee will work within a budget that will not place a financial burden on the Church membership.

God requires wise stewardship in all Church matters. It is especially true when it comes to the spending of money. Mature Christian trustees are worth their weight in gold. It is important for a church to be guided by the Holy Spirit and Prayer when selecting trustees.

SPECIFIC DUTIES OF THE TRUSTEE

---

*Supervise Financial Matters
*Oversee Facility Maintenance
*Seek Legal Service When Necessary

- Arrange for major and minor repairs to the physical facilities of the church
- Advise the church on the need for improvements on the real estate holdings of the church
- Represent the church concerning legal matters
- Help draft the church budget

It is advised that trustees seek legal advice to be sure of all the legal ramifications whenever signing major legal documents such as stocks, bonds, mortgages, etc. Traditionally it has been a practice for only three to sign legal documents.[2]

QUALIFICATIONS

There are no specific biblical qualifications for a trustee, because it is not a scriptural office. Most churches use the same qualifications mentioned for deacons in the selection of trustees. Those qualifications are recorded in Acts 6:3-5 and 1 Timothy 3:3-13.

Selection Process

Trustees are selected much in the same way as deacons. The pastor, trustees or church members recommend potential candidates. Many churches choose candidates who have a strong business background who meet the biblical standards found in Acts the 6th chapter.

Selecting a candidate who has a keen sense of purpose and direction is well advised. Proven leadership and sound Christian commitment are two criterions that should not be compromised in the selection process.

It is important to screen each candidate very carefully, because the future direction of the church financial operations is strongly influenced by the trustees. It would be wise to select candidates who use sound, patient judgment before making final decisions on matters concerning the church.

Honesty cannot be over emphasized. The person who is chosen to be a trustee is trusted with the financial matters of the church. Honesty must be the trademark of the trustee if the church is to meet its' full financial obligations.

Finally, the pastor and the trustees usually interview the candidate who meets the standards to be a trustee. If approved, he's brought before the church and voted on. Some churches may have a diverse selection process.

Church Trustee Qualities

- Salvation (A trustee must be saved; the blind cannot lead the blind.)
- Constant prayer is essential in a trustee's life
- A sense of dedication (A trustee must have a sense of purpose and have the will to achieve stated goals and objectives.)
- An unselfish Spirit of Love (A trustee must possess a sense of love for God and their fellow man.)
- A Spirit of Service and Humility (A trustee must be willing to work toward improving the welfare of others.)
- A Spiritual Vision (A church must possess a hunger for righteousness and a vision to up build the kingdom of God.)
- Written Goals and Objectives (Clearly defined goals and objectives are essential to trustee work.)
- An Action Plan (A trustee must have an effective action plan.)
- A trustee should possess a knowledge of budgeting and proper money usage

The work of the trustee is needed in the Contemporary Church more than ever. We live in world where people are suing others at a high rate. Some people are seeking financial gain through senseless lawsuits. The church is a potential target for money scams. It is important that trustees seek legal advice to protect themselves and the church from those who seek to benefit from suing the church for hefty sums of money.

It is important to update the Church Constitutions and by laws to make sure that the documents are current if the church enter legal litigation. It is extremely important to have well-informed persons on the Trustee Ministry.

There are times when churches have allowed nonmembers who are Christians to serve on their Trustee Ministry. This is not an endorsement to allow nonmember to serve as trustees. I am sharing this information to make churches aware that they need to have knowledgeable trustees who have the skills to perform the duties of trustees. If a church allows a nonmember to serve on their Trustee Ministry, it is suggested that seventy-five percentage of the trustees be members of that church.

Sample Youth Program

SAMPLE YOUTH PROGRAM

Spiritual Training of Youth is Essential for the Survival of the Church

---

A strong youth program is essential to the spiritual and social development of youth in the local church. The youth director is encouraged to work in cooperation with the pastor, the staff, and other committed parishioners to assure that the spiritual needs of the youth and children are addressed in a comprehensive youth program.

Sample Objectives: Youth Program

Theme: Building Christian Character

The main goal of a Christian Youth Program is to provide guidance and leadership to youth (assisting them to develop strong Christian character.)

Objectives:

- to lead youth to a commitment to Jesus Christ as Lord and Savior
- to involve them in responsible church membership and participation in the life of the denomination
- to provide activities at church for worship, discussions, bible study, social life, witness and ministry
- to help the youth to become responsible, accountable, rational beings
- to involve the youth in a variety of Christian activities

- to provide the youth with a strong Christian model
- to expose the youth to the different phrases of Christian ministries
- to help the youth get their priorities straight
- to give youth an opportunity to fully develop their talents
- to encourage the youth to do their best at all times
- to encourage them to become active participants in Christian stewardship and not just spectators

PROJECTED YOUTH ACTIVITIES

- drama productions
- oratory contests
- sports participation
- creative writing projects
- talent contests
- music therapy
- debating teams
- community projects
- prayer teams
- dinner fellowships
- poetry therapy
- group games
- arts and crafts
- teaching opportunities
- group visitation
- group picnics
- bible study
- attend conferences
- rap sessions
- worship services

RESPONSIBILITIES OF THE LEADER AND COUNSELORS

Youth leaders should be responsible, accountable Christians. They should also enjoy working with youth. The number one priority of a youth leader should be to spread the teachings of Jesus Christ.

Three things to Remember as a Youth Leader

- lead by word and action
- know how and when to set limits
- be dedicated and committed
- cooperation with the pastor and other committees:

Teamwork is Essential in Christian Service

The Pastor Should be Informed of All Youth Activities to Avoid a Conflict of Interests

The following Youth Leader Guide was modeled after the 1982 Brochure "Organizing A Baptist Student Union "by the National Student Ministries of Nashville, Tennessee

LEADER	DUTIES
President	Presides over meetings; works directly with the youth director; aids in planning, coordinating, directing and evaluating the overall youth program; provides for promotion, records, finances, enlistment and involvement of youth
Vice President	Assist the president in promotion, publicity, communication and public relations and acts as the presiding officer in the absence of the president
Secretary	Keeps a system of the program's records; minutes of each meeting; records minutes of each meeting; serves as the correspondent or agent of the youth group
Treasurer	Receives offerings and special gifts; deposit all monies in an authorized account; post receipts and disbursements of all accounts prepare financial

reports for group accounting; signs all checks; maintains financial records in safe place

Christian Character

Chairperson   Leads in:

- Christian growth workshops
- Bible study
- Worship (individual & group)
- Current event discussions
- Social and fellowship activities
- Promote recreational involvement
- Help build good child/parent relationships

Chairperson   Promote youth missions; develop opportunities for ministry to non-Christians; encourage youth to get involved in community projects which would aid the needy; assist youth in their personal needs and concern

Director   The director is the person secured by the pastor and church membership or the local youth work committee to provide adult guidance and supervision of the youth program

Executive Committee:

The executive committee is made of the different leaders within the youth program.

- **Administration and Support Leaders**
- Pastor
- President
- Vice President
- Promotion Chairperson
- Enrollment Chairperson
- Records and Finance Chairperson
- Christian Character Leaders
- Christian Growth Chairperson
- Fellowship and Social Events Chairperson

- Study Chairperson
- Worship Chairperson
- Stewardship and Missions Person
- Christian Sharing Leaders
- Witness and Missions Chairperson
- Social Involvement Chairperson
- Evangelistic Chairperson

Meetings:

- All committee meetings will open with a prayer and devotion.
- The committee will meet on days designated by the individual members of each organization.
- Meeting days of the committee will be used for planning and discussion

Meeting Dates of the Youth Executive Committee:

A specific date or days will be decided on and voted on by the committee.

Promotion:

The Executive Committee should promote the youth program, along with the pastor and church members.

Financial Support:

The state conventions, churches and those who make special donations support youth programs.

Pastor Relationship:

All committees should work in conjunction with the pastor and the membership to provide a comprehensive youth program for the purpose of building strong Christian character.

IDENTIFYING NEEDS

Each church should identify youth development needs and work toward satisfying those needs. Churches that implements an effective youth program are blessed because a youth program usually produces a wealth of positive fruit, which extends beyond the boundaries of the church for its' effects are generally felt in the community and other spheres of life.

As previously mentioned, all church organizations should have a knowledge of how to identify needs in their prospective programs. This is especially true in the youth program because the youth are our most valuable resource.

A church can identify youth developmental needs in the same way that they identify other church needs:

- written survey
- question and answer sheet
- personal conversation

All the above are great ways to identify youth program needs, but perhaps the most effective way of identifying youth program needs is to alert the Christian Education Ministry members and other responsible church members to report perceived needs to the church officials on a regular basis. Some standard youth development needs are:

- prayer and quiet time needs
- bible study needs
- recreational needs
- current event discussions
- Christian growth discussions

YOUTH GOALS AND OBJECTIVES

When youth development needs in a church are adequately listed and identified, the youth committee should write clear, precise, goals and objectives, and draft an action plan on how these goals and objectives will be achieved.

Many youth programs are ineffective because of the failure to follow through in achieving desired goals and objectives. One of the ways to monitor the progress of achieving goals and objectives is to schedule regular update reports. These reports will eliminate a lot of guesswork on which goals and objectives are being met and serve as a guide for the Board members to periodically modify strategies to increase desired program effectiveness.

There are times when the wrong goals and objectives are set for a youth program. When this is apparent, the Youth Ministry should recognize the problem and make the necessary corrections. As mentioned, many churches have lost valuable time by working on goals and objectives that were irrelevant to their Christian education needs. Time is too important and too precious to be wasted on irrelevant goals and objectives. There is simply too much to be accomplished in the church and too many precious lives are affected.

As previously mentioned, it is important to have goals because they:

- help leaders to determine the form and content of the teaching program.
- provide leaders with a sense of direction and a means of charting progress.
- offer a framework for evaluating the achievements of the overall teaching aim.

AGE GROUPS

The psychology of age groups is an area that every person in youth ministry should be aware of because each age group has specific needs that must be addressed if any genuine Christian education is to take place.

It would benefit teachers to have a knowledge of the emotional make up of their pupils. The teacher who possess such a knowledge is better equipped to acquire and retain the interests' level of those they work with.

Things to remember in working with children

Stay Focused and Give Your Best When Working with Children They Are Our Most Precious Resource

---

- Speak to them on their level
- Allow sufficient recess time
- Speak low and plain so you will be understood
- Have plenty of space
- Use music at various intervals in the teaching process
- Assign individual and group projects that will require children to work with their hands.
- Encourage the children to repeat given cheers and phrases.
- Give verbal rewards when necessary.
- Give children an opportunity to demonstrate a given talent if they desire to do so.
- Listen to what children have to say.
- Be conscious of body language.

Things to remember in working with Youth

Be Loving, Kind and Patient, and Maintain a Sense of Purpose, and Stay Focused

---

- Use role-playing or drama as a teaching instrument.
- Make use of audio visual aids.
- Assign group activities
- Encourage constructive competition among the youth and send delegates to state conventions
- Plan youth retreats and workshops on relevant youth issues.
- Have panel discussions.
- Assign projects.
- Have talent shows.
- Play group games.
- Have reward banquets

Parts Adopted from: Organizing and Maintaining a Baptist Student Union Bulletin 1983 Nashville, Tennessee.

Suggestions on Maintaining a Good Youth Program:

Preparation, Hard Work, Patience, Kindness and a willingness to Be Led by the Holy Spirit Are Keys to a Successful Youth Program

---

- Make sure that the youth program meetings are interesting. One way to kill a youth program is to have dull, uninteresting speakers or activities. The youth program committee should make sure that the meetings are interesting and that they address the spiritual needs of the youth.
- Give each youth some responsibility. It could be an appointment to serve on a special program committee or a request to work on a special research assignment.
- Encourage youth to participate in recreation. For example, the entire youth group could participate as a team in playing basketball, football, bowling, skating, or fellowship during special event activity.
- Fellowship with other church groups
- Organize a Youth Council, which meets on a regular basis throughout the year
- Send youth to State and National Youth Conferences and Conventions.
- Write clear, precise goals and objectives, and state specific times for achieving desired results.
- Organize a youth choir, which sings on a designated Sunday and participates on programs at different churches.
- Show concern for special holidays and sponsor special events.
- Maintain good public relations with other organizations within the church.
- Pray for the guidance of the Holy Spirit and promote Christian love.

Special Projects – including fund raising

The youth program must always be alive and creative, with a variety of innovative ideas. Some tithing churches do not need youth fund raising programs but for those churches that choose to raise funds the following is a list of fundraising suggestions.

They Include:

- bake sales
- car washes
- pre-Christmas bazaar (holiday bazaar)
- garage sales
- gospel program (concerts)
- ask businessmen to sponsor certain projects
- candy sales
- faculty talent show (talent and fashion shows)
- churches should budget money for youth programs
- individual donations to the youth program

SAMPLE OF A YOUTH BIBLICAL NAME GAME

Opening Statement: "I have something that may be of interest, it is called the Name Game. Feel free to participate, you might surprise yourself. For example, I will describe a biblical character, and you are to name the character. Everyone is encouraged to participate."

Who Was I?

1.
   - I was a Jew...born in Tarsus in Ci-li-ci-a.
   - I persecuted the church.
   - I was blinded on the road to Damascus.

   - Who was I?..........Paul..........Acts 9 and Acts 22

2.
   - I suffered many trials and tribulations.
   - I had a wife, seven sons and three daughters.
   - I was a rich man who had lots of animals.
   - I am known best for overcoming great suffering.

   - Who was I?..........Job..........Job 1:1-6

3.
   - I was a man full of faith and of the Holy Ghost.
   - I stood up for Jesus and spoke boldly of him in the mist of the Pharisees and Sadducees.

- When they stoned me, I asked God to have mercy on them.
- I was one of the original Deacons.

- Who was I?..........Stephen..........Acts 6

4.
- I was called the child of promise; my father was a well-known biblical character.
- I have two sons who were also well known biblical characters
- one of them wrestled with an angel.

- Who was I?..........Isaac..........Genesis 24 and 27

5.
- I was one of the twelve disciples.
- I was the son of a fisherman.
- I am referred to as the disciple whom Jesus loved.

- Who was I?..........John..........Matthew 4

6.
- The city I lived in was very wicked and sinful.
- My uncle was a great Patriarch.
- The city I lived in was destroyed and my wife disobeyed God.

- Who was I?..........Lot..........Genesis 13

7.
- I was a Pharisee and a ruler of the Jews.
- I came to the master by night, because I was a shame to come by day.
- I asked a question about the new life.

- Who was I?..........Nicodemus..........John 3

8.
- I was a rebel.
- I burned down Roman cities.
- I was imprisoned and released because they chose to spare my life.

- Who was I?..........Ba-rab-bas..........Matthew 27:17-26

9. • I lived 930 years.
   • I named each animal in God's kingdom.
   • Some people say that I caused sin to come into the world.

   • Who was I?..........Adam..........Genesis 2:7-21; Genesis 3:17-20; Genesis 5:3-5

10. • I was called the forerunner of Jesus Christ.
    • I had my own disciples.
    • I was the cousin of Jesus Christ

    • Who was I?..........John the Baptist..........Luke 1; Matthew 3:1-15

Where Was I?

1. • I was a place where wicked men and women lived.
   • Angels visited me.
   • Fire and brimstone rained down on me.

   • Where was I?..........Sodom and Gomorrah.......... Genesis 13:10-12

2. • Two trees were planted in the midst of me.
   • I was known as a Paradise.
   • I was a garden.

   • Where was I?..........Garden of Eden..........Genesis 2:8-15

3. I am either known as a mountain or as a desert.
   • I became very famous when the Hebrews came out of Egyptian slavery.
   • A very important event took place on me.

   • Where was I?..........Mt. Sinai..........Exodus 19 and 20

4. I am the place where a very rich man lived.
   • He was said to be one of the richest men who lived in the East.
   • I am the place where a lot of suffering took place.

   • Where was I?..........The Land of Uz..........Job 1:1

5. I am the place of a very important meeting between Jesus and his cousin.
    *   I am a very important body of water.
    *   I am the place where Naaman the Leper was healed.

    *   Where was I?..........The Jordan River.......II Kings 5; Matthew 3:1-5

6. I was an isolated place.
    *   I am the place where the beloved disciple of Jesus was exiled.
    *   I am an island.

    *   Where was I?..........Isle of Patmos..........Revelations 1:9

7. I am a hill outside of Jerusalem.
    *   I am referred to as the place of the skull.
    *   Jesus was crucified here.

    *   Where was I?..........Golgotha..........John 19:17

8. I am a city and I was conquered by David.
    *   Nebuchadnezzar destroyed me.
    *   Cyrus rebuilt me.
    *   I am perhaps the most famous city in the world.

    *   Where was I?..........Jerusalem..........II Samuel 5:6-7

9. Rahab lived there.
    *   Spies were sent to bring back information.
    *   I am the city where a very important battle was fought.

    *   Where was I?..........Jericho..........Joshua 2:1-15; Joshua 6:1-26

10. I was much traveled in ancient biblical times.
    *   I was a very famous road.
    *   I am the road that the Apostle Paul was converted on.

    *   Where was I?..........The Damascus Road..........Acts 9:3-20

151

What A m I?

1. I was made of gopher wood.
   - I helped both men and beast find their way to safety.
   - I was rained on for 40 days and 40 nights.

   - What am I?..........Noah's ark..........Genesis 6 and 7

2. I was built with brick and stone.
   - The people who built me were very proud.
   - Before I was built the whole earth was of one language and of one speech.

   - What am I?..........The Tower of Babel..........Genesis 11

3. James talked about me.
   - I have caused much joy and lots of pain.
   - I am one of the smallest members of the body, yet I am very powerful.

   - What am I?..........The Tongue..........1st chapter of James

4. I was used by the Roman government.
   - I was a symbol of evil to the Roman government, but a symbol of hope and salvation to mankind.
   - I have a very distinct shape.

   - What am I?..........The cross..........I Corinthians 1:17

5. I am a symbol of glory.
   - Priests and kings wore me.
   - The bible says the righteous shall receive me when the chief appears.

   - What am I?..........A crown..........I Corinthians 9:25; I Peter 5:4; II Timothy 4:8

6. I serve a very important function in Christian worship.
    - The disciples observed me.
    - I am known by two very distinct symbols.

    - What am I?..........The Lord's Supper..........I Corinthians 11:20-29

7. I am an ancient ceremony.
    - I symbolize the new life.
    - A man in the wilderness performed me.

    - What am I?..........Baptism..........Mark 1:1-5

8. I have caused a lot of pain and heartache
    - I am universal, everyone is affected by me.
    - I cause people to feel guilty.

    - What am I?.........Sin.........Genesis 3:1-8; Romans 3:23; Psalms 51:5

9. I bring people together.
    - Jesus constantly talked about me.
    - I am discussed in John 3:16.

    - What am I?..........Love..........I Corinthians 13

10. I am a product of the most powerful force in the world.
    - People who possess me are better equipped to live the Christian life.
    - Paul discussed me in Galatians.

    - What am I?..........The Fruit of the Spirit..........Galatians 5:22-25

The Scripture says train a child when he is young and when he is old he will not depart from it. There is a window of opportunity in every child's life when impressions are permanently seared into their consciousness. It is important that these impressions be positive experiences, which will serve as a foundation for Christian Character and Spiritual Growth

Suggested Monthly Youth Activities

These suggested monthly youth activities are not designed to conflict with the established youth programs within an organization. Churches and other organizations are encouraged to plan their own monthly activities if they so desire. The idea is to highlight the importance of youth as the nation's most precious resource.

January

Values Education Month
Highlight the importance of good citizenship, and Christian values

February

Buffet Food

Heritage Education Month
Treat the youth to a buffet dinner, show heritage videos, share heritage information, etc.

March

Entertainment Month
Sponsor a trip to the movies or family entertainment

April

Armed Services Month
Encourage the youth to send cards or write letters to those who serve in the armed forces

May

Travel Month
Sponsor an out of town trip

June

Health Education Month
Invite a health professional to come and discuss ways to remain healthy

July

Joint Activities Faith Month
Plan an activity with another Church or organization, place emphasis on religious training

August

Education Month
Invite educators to discuss ways to succeed in the school system or host a mathematics or language arts seminar

September

Sports Month
As a group, attend a local or out of town sporting event

October

Law Enforcement Month
Partner with other churches or organizations in the area and invite law enforcement officers to come and discuss ways to avoid drugs, alcohol and sexual predators

November

Parent Appreciation Month
Encourage youth to make cards or save money to buy their parents a gift or to take them out to dinner

December

Giving, Sharing, Talent Expression / Award Appreciation Month
Highlight the importance of giving to those who are less fortunate, emphasize the importance of positive relationships, plan an awards/certificate program with other churches or organizations and allow the youth to display their talents such as art, singing, building, and writing etc., host an appreciation meal, summarize the year, allow youth to discuss the highlights of the year

Promote Power Point Projects where youth make power points on the Fruit of the Spirit and other biblical themes.

It is the Little Things that Matters the most in a Child's Life

Most psychologists agree that the first 6 years of a child's life is when their mood and temperament is cultivated and developed. There is a saying "A person's attitude will determine their altitude in life." Therefore, it is important for parents to cultivate a caring loving home environment.

Children mimic the mood and the behavior of their parents; therefore, it is important for parents to speak and behave in a positive way when interacting with children. When there is a balance of praise and constructive criticism in the early years of a child's life, a spirit of confidence and self-worth is usually infused.

Children are the future doctors, lawyers, teachers, nurses, barbers, mechanics and rest home attendants, they are leaders in training. The next Dr. King or Dr. Graham may be residing in someone's home. Therefore, it is important for parents to be positive role models.

It is the little things that matters the most in a child's life. It is those times when the television is turned off, or a newspaper is cast aside to listen to what is being said. Children value loving caring relationships and words of encouragement more than they value expensive toys.

The time spent attending a tennis match, a basketball game or the time taken out of a busy schedule to attend church or a dance recital is more valuable than silver or gold. Spending quality time with children is essential for their physical and spiritual development.

It is the love that is shown to a child that matters the most, it is the tears of joy when they take their first steps or speak their first words but most important of all it is the prayers and hugs they receive as they grow from infancy to maturity.

The little things that we do for our children will determine the important things that they do in life. Let us nurture and develop a renewed Spirit of love, peace and hope for our nation's youth.

It is time to equip our youth to survive in a global society

Some feel that other countries are the greatest threats to their national security, this may be true but the failure to equip children and youth with the knowledge on how to survive in a global society may be the greatest threat of the present age.

Drug abuse and the rise of sexually transmitted diseases; such as Aids is an indication that the media, the home and the religious community has failed to communicate the true dangers of drug abuse and the deadly effects of illicit sexually activity.

Some Contemporary Churches seems to be asleep at the wheel when it comes to addressing youth issues and concerns. Today's church will awake one day and realize that insufficient information and education are factors that have devastated the lives of countless young people. Statistics indicate that children respond to effective teaching programs whether they be in our churches or schools.

Numerous movies glorify drug abuse and illicit sexual activity to the point where the consequences and the stigma of the behavior has been detached for increasing profits. A disconnect between fantasy and reality has trapped many young people into an endless cycle of drug dependency and sexual immorality.

Positive information that impact the lives of youth is essential in he this Social Media society. Young people need to know how to avoid sexual predators because there is an alarming increase of sexual offenders. Unfortunately, the danger of sexual predators is usually only emphasized when an innocent child has been killed or kidnapped. It is time for the media, the church, and the family to switch from being reactive to proactive when discussing sexual predators, for instances children need to know the profile of sexual predators which is usually a normal looking person who looks like the person who lives next door.

The abuse of children has gotten out of hand, it is time to do some soul searching and research to find out why grown men and women feel that it okay to sexually abuse children. Switching from being reactive to proactive in addressing the sexual predator issues will go a long way toward to making young people more aware of sexual predators. Reacting when a tragedy occurs has been the standard in far too long.

When young people become victims of sexual predators and drug abuse the future of mankind is at stake. The church can no longer take for granted that young people will become productive citizens in a society which expose youth to mature experiences which they are unable to handle emotionally.

It is time to make children aware that evil exists in the world and it is a real force that impacts the lives of people. Children need to know that they have the power to avoid drugs, sexually transmitted diseases and in many cases, they can avoid sexual predators, one of the keys is to make healthy life style healthy choices, learn the words of prayer and discuss their fears and concerns with their parents or school officials.

Sample Youth Worship Service

SAMPLE YOUTH WORSHIP SERVICE OUTLINE

Musical Prelude ....Musician
Call to Worship...Short Prayer
Special Music ....Choir
Christian Poetry...Youth Reader
Hymn ....Choir
Scripture...Youth Reader
Prayer ....Youth Reader
Response. ....Choir
Responsive Character Statement ....Leader
Mission Prayer/Offering ....Ushers
Special Tribute ....Leader
Congregational Hymn ....Choir
Introduction of Speaker ....Leader
Inspirational Selection ....Choir
Address..Minister
Invitational Hymn ....Choir
Remarks ....Open
Benediction...Minister

SAMPLE: YOUTH WORSHIP SERVICE

Musical Prelude ....Musician
Call to Worship...Short Prayer

28 Come unto me, all ye that labour and are heavy laden, and I will give you rest. 29 Take my yoke upon you, and learn of me; for I am meek and lowly in heart: and ye shall find rest unto your souls. 30 For my yoke is easy, and my burden is light. (Matthew 11:28-30)

Special Music ....Choir

Hymn of fellowship "O Be Joyful in the Lord!"

Christian Poetry...Youth Reader

The Beauty of Language

To me poetry is a language of beauty:

A. And some of the most beautiful poetry is found in the Bible.
B. In turning to Psalm 23 we find a classical example of poetry inspired by God.
C. It is spoken in such a beautiful language, that if it's read with any degree of interests it will bring sunshine on an overcast day.

O' David must have had a strong belief in the Lord when he wrote "The Lord is my shepherd; I shall not want..." Can you see the beauty of the language and the hidden meaning of the verse? For a shepherd is one who feeds and protects his flock.

David goes on to say "He maketh me to lie down in green pastures; he leadeth me beside the still waters." In other words, in times of trials and tribulations, he brings rest, peace and serenity.

"He restoreth my soul; he leadeth me in the paths of righteousness for his name's sake." David says in a sense he gives me energy, and directs me to the right way of life. Can you see the beauty?

"Yea, though I walk through the valley of the shadow of death. I will fear no Evil; for thou art with me; thy rod and thy staff they comfort me." In this verse we see the intensity of David's relationship with the Lord. When he says I have no fears, death cannot harm me and I know that God loves me because he chastises those whom he love.

By this time David is completely comforted and he has no fears of this world nor of the world to come.

As he writes, "Thou prepare a table before me in the presence of mine Enemies; thou anoint my head with oil, my cup run over." We see that all of David's earthly needs have been met; he is completely satisfied with the Grace of God.

He is ready to go home now as he writes, "Surely, goodness and mercy shall follow me all the days of my life and I will dwell in the house of the Lord Forever."

Hymn ....Choir "How Sweet the Name of Jesus"
Scripture...Youth Reader

He that committeth sin is of the devil; for the devil sinneth from the beginning. For this purpose, the Son of God was manifested that he might destroy the works of the devil. (I John 3:8) (KJV)

Prayer ....Youth

Eternal and all wise, God who created the heavens and the earth, let your love reign supreme in the hearts of all who are present, through Jesus Christ our Lord, Amen.

Response ....Choir

Doxology

Responsive Character Statement

Leader: What is true Christian character?

Youth: It is love, joy, peace, long-suffering,gentleness, goodness, faith, meekness and temperance.

Leader: How does a person acquire Christian character?

Youth: Through faith in Jesus, Christian fellowship, worship and prayer

Leader: Who is in control of Christian character?

Youth: The Holy Spirit is in control.

Leader: What does strong Christian character produce?

Youth: It produces patience, love, peace, strength and courage.

Leader: Why is Christian character so important?

Youth: It is important because it inspires others & promotes positive behavior patterns & relationships.

Leader: Who needs strong Christian character?

Youth: Everyone needs to possess a strong Christian character.

Leader: Why does everyone need to possess a strong Christian character?

Youth: Because if everyone possessed a strong Christian character there would be no strife, hatred or envy. There would only be peace, love, fellowship and joy.

All: Let's strive to develop strong Christian character in our own personal lives, for in doing so the world will be a better place to live in.

Mission Prayer ....Ushers

Father, we pray that you will take this offering and use it for the up building of your kingdom. Amen.

Mission Offering ....Ushers
Special Tribute ....Leader

A special speech or song.

Congregational Hymn ....Choir

"How Sweet the Name of Jesus"

Introduction of Speaker ....Leader
Inspirational Selection ....Choir

"Reach Out and Touch"

Address..Minister

Sermon: The Tragedy of Macbeth

Maybe one of the most tragic human experiences is the loss of self-control. Macbeth became a victim of personal ambition and desire because he lost respect for human life and allowed his dreams of power and control to dominate his thoughts. I am reminded of the serpent in the creation story who persuaded Eve to eat of the tree of good and evil. A thought was planted in the mind of Eve that she could be like God.

The same kind of thought was placed in victorious Macbeth as he and Banquo returned from battle. Three witches on a desolate heath greeted Macbeth as Thane of Glamis, Thane of Cawdor, and "King hereafter." The desire to be great and important was probably always within the nature of Macbeth, but it had not blossomed into a full force.

The prophecy of the three witches seem to have reinforced what Macbeth desired to be all along. He wanted to be a king and to have a lot of wealth and power. The tragic thing about wealth and power is that it corrupts when it is abused. Many men down through history have been destroyed by wealth and power because they fail to realize that earthly wealth and power is temporary for it guarantees no lasting joy and happiness.

Alexander the Great is a classic example of a man who became disillusion with power and wealth. It is said that he conquered all of the known world but sat down and cried like a baby because he had no more worlds to conquer. He discovered that power and wealth brings no lasting satisfaction.

The tragedy of Macbeth is magnified when he learns that Duncan's son Malcolm had been appointed Prince of Cumberland, the automatic successor to the throne. It is at this point that Macbeth entertains the thought of killing the king.

Satan has a way of reinforcing evil thoughts in the hearts of people. He was able to reinforce evil intentions within Macbeth through his wife, Lady Macbeth, when she questioned his courage and his desire to become king. Lady Macbeth was as cold-blooded as Jezebel. She had no respect for human life. She thought only of her personal pleasure and desire. She saw Macbeth as a medium through which she could realize her own personal desire for wealth and power.

The total bankruptcy of Macbeth is magnified when he arranges to have his closest friend, Banquo, murdered because Banquo suspected him of murdering Duncan. Macbeth had reached a desperate stage in his life where he no longer trusted anyone. He had become an isolated man who was a victim of his own selfish goals and desires. He had no one other than his wife, Lady Macbeth, to share his wealth and power. The tragedy of Macbeth is further magnified when Lady Macbeth was driven to insanity and eventually committed suicide.

Lady Macbeth simply reached the end of the rope. She could not control the fear and remorse that eventually totally dominated her thoughts. The death of Lady Macbeth marked the total isolation of Macbeth. He had no one to share his goals and ambitions with.

The sins of Macbeth began to haunt him more and more. Sin has a way of isolating a man to the point where he is no longer in fellowship with God. In the case of Macbeth, sin had driven him to a degraded state. It was one murder after the other. He was determined to destroy all of his opposition because he felt that his life had to be protected at all cost.

Macbeth is a classic example of what a Christian should not be, for he loved himself more than he loved others. He made no personal sacrifices for the welfare of others.

Jesus Christ was the one who denied himself by giving his life on the cross. He knew that true happiness is found in serving others.

Macbeth's earthly desire to remain in power and control drove him to seek advice from the supernatural who was represented by the three witches. He wanted some assurances that things would get better in his life. But, after meeting with the three witches, things got worse for the ghostly appearances of an armored head warned him against Macduff. It was Macduff who was born not of woman who would eventually bring an end to Macbeth.

Macbeth responded to Macduff in a very sinful way. He set out to control his own destiny by attempting to destroy Macduff. Sin says if you cannot destroy your intended target, destroy the closest thing around it. Thus, Macbeth had his loyalist to assassinate Macduff's family because Macduff had escaped to England.

Murder and deception had become a way of life for Macbeth. What started out, as blind ambition became hopelessness and frustration. Macbeth reached a point where he no longer could see a rainbow of many colors, for he could only see distrust, dismay and doom.

Macbeth became like Satan. He was as a drowning man with little hope of his spirits being resurrected. His life was full of misery. He had no love to give, therefore, he gave none. He had become as an animal who's only concern was survival. It was hard for him to keep his head above the water. He had to devour others to stay afloat.

What a sad commentary of life when one's survival depends upon the destruction of others.

The emptiness of Macbeth's accomplishments are magnified in his words "Life is a tale told by an idiot, full of sound and fiery signifying nothing." Life had become a burden to Macbeth.

Macbeth no longer had a true meaning or purpose in life. His riches and his status as king no longer brought satisfaction and fulfillment. Macbeth had become totally enslaved by sin. At first the fruits of sin were sweet, but now with age the fruits of sin had turned bitter and sour.

Man; in his finite state have a beginning and an end. The man who depends upon his own personal goals and ambitions for happiness usually reaps sadness and destruction. But, the man who depends upon the infinite love and everlasting joy of Jesus Christ reaps peace and happiness, for the Bible says "the whole duty of man is to serve God."

Macbeth's hopes were built upon the sandy foundation of an earthly kingship. Like all earthly substances they pass away with the passing of time, but heavenly aspirations which supersede earthly time and matter will last forever.

The grand and noble spirit of Jesus Christ was not in the life of **Macbeth as a guiding force. Macbeth navigated his life through his personal will and determination. The tragedy of the personal navigation of his life rests in the fact that sinful desires caused Macbeth to steer the course of his life in the wrong direction. Sin is a one way street that leads to pain and destruction.**

Macbeth, like all men, was totally helpless to change the course of his life. No man can pull himself up by his bootstraps and totally change the course of his life. Man, who is created in the image of God, must realize that he is not in total control of his life's existence. For the fact of the matter is that God is ultimately in control of all things.

The central theme of the Bible is portrayed in the story of Macbeth. That is, that good will ultimately triumph over evil, for God will usually have a ram in the bush to accomplish his purpose.

Just as Moses was used as an instrument to free the children of Israel, it can be said that Macduff was used as an instrument to bring about the liberation of Scotland. Macduff was in a sense a ram in the bush. He came to the defense of Scotland in her darkest hour. It was Macduff who left his family unguarded in order to seek out Malcolm and prepare a defense against Macbeth.

Macduff's patriotism was neither greedy nor self-serving. This is the kind of loyalty and patriotism that characterizes the Christian character. For true Christian character inspires a person to a sense of sincere loyalty even to the point of sacrifice and loss. In the case of Macduff, it was the loss of family. I am inclined to believe had Macduff had knew beforehand that he was going to lose his family, he would have still given all to liberate Scotland.

We know in the Christian faith that Jesus Christ gave his life to save the souls of dying men and women, for he knew that there was no sacrifice too great to save the souls of dying men and women.

Macduff, in his quest, reminded me of David as he did battle against Goliath. David knew that Goliath was a giant who possessed great strength and power. He confronted Goliath bold and unafraid, because he was filled with the spirit of God. He had a sense of purpose. He believed in his heart that he would be victorious **against Goliath.**

Macduff likewise, in his quest against Macbeth, knew that Macbeth had claimed supernatural power, that no man born of woman could destroy him. The fact that Macduff was born caesarian does not decrease the amount of courage and boldness it took for him to stand against Macbeth. It took a great deal of courage on his part because his own personal life was at stake. He could have just as easily been the victim rather than the victor in his confrontation with Macbeth.

The confrontation of Macduff against Macbeth bore similarities to the great confrontation that took place in heaven between Satan and Michael. It was a confrontation between good and evil. Michael waged war against Satan and his forces and caste them out of heaven. Macduff waged war against Macbeth destroying him in the process. Good will triumph over evil is the hope of the Christian.

CONCLUSION

The story of Macbeth is a story of life. The characters portrayed symbolized the many struggles of life. Each character was a player who affected each other's thoughts and actions. Ross, the messenger who brought the good news of Macbeth's military victory and bad news about his family, was a role player.

Lennox, the noble who accompanied Macbeth to the dead king's chambers and who grew increasingly sarcastic and fearful for the fate of Scotland, was indeed role player.

The porter, the keeper of Macbeth's castle who drunkenly imagined that he was the keeper of Hell's Gate, was a role player. Those who read the tragedy of Macbeth are also role players. It is their role to preach and teach against wickedness and injustice.

Christians must promote the goals and objectives of the Christian faith and not their personal goals and objectives.

And God shall wipe away all tears from their eyes, and there shall be no more death, neither sorrow, nor crying, neither shall there be any more pain; for the former things are passed away. Revelations 21:4 (KJV)

    Invitational Hymn ....Choir
    Remarks ....Open
    Benediction..Minister

May the love of God and the peace of Jesus Christ continue to be with each one of you.

Sample Youth Constitution

Constitution of the Youth Association of Mount Calvary Church

Preamble

We, the youth of Mount Calvary Church, in order to establish a more effective youth counsel, and to bring about a greater working relationship with the church and with its' officers and to promote responsibility, self-control and loyalty, and to keep the social activities of our group in harmony with church standards, do with the co-operation of the church hereby adopt the following constitution:

Constitution

Article I - Name

The name of this organization shall be The Youth Association of Mount Calvary Church.

Article II - Objectives

The objectives of The Youth Association are stated in the Preamble of this Constitution.

Article III - Membership and Organization

Section A - This association shall be composed of all youth ages 13 to 21 years.

Section B - The branches of the Youth Association shall consist of an Advisory and an Executive Body.

Article IV – Amendments

Section A - Proposal

- The Advisory Ministry (which is the Executive Body)or any member of the organization can submit a proposed amendment.
- The proposed amendment can be submitted to the Executive Body by petitions bearing the names of 75% of the members.
- Two weeks written notice must be given to the Executive Body prior to the legislation.

Section B - Ratification and Approval

- To ratify the amendment a 2/3 affirmative vote in which 75% of the member participation shall be required.
- The ratified amendment shall then be forwarded to the Executive Body of the organization for approval.

Article V - General Officers

The officers of The Youth Association of Mount Calvary Church shall be the President, Vice President, Secretary and Treasurer.

Article VI - Powers

Section A - The advisory and executive ministries shall have disciplinary power over the youth body in areas designated by this constitution and its' by-laws.

Section B - The advisory and executive ministries shall have the power to make such legislation, resolutions, recommendations and endorsements as it deems necessary to fulfill the responsibilities and duties set forth in this constitution and its' by-laws.

Article VII - Executive Body

Section A - Members

- Any executive power delegated shall be vested in the President of the Youth Association.
- The Executive Body of the association shall be the President, Vice President, Secretary and Treasurer. These officers shall be elected during a specific time and in a manner fixed by the by-laws of the Youth Association and shall hold the office for a term of one year provided that eligibility for the office is maintained or until their successors are elected and qualified.

Section B - President

- The President of the Executive Body should be responsible and competent.
- There shall be no sex discrimination; the president can be male or female

Authority and duties:

- The President of the Association shall preside over all meetings of the Youth Association.
- The President of the Association shall have authority to veto or approve legislation of the Youth Association
- A veto may be overridden by a majority vote of 3/4 of the membership of the Youth Association
- Failure to veto legislation within 7 days following the suggestion constitutes approval.

. The President of the Association may recommend legislation for Consideration

- The President may call the Youth Association into a special session with proper notice.
- The President of the Association or his appointee shall represent the association at all functions where association is expected to officially represent.

Section C - Vice President

The qualifications of the Vice President shall be the same as those specified for the President

Authority and Duties:

- The Vice President shall be the chairperson of the Youth Association and preside in the absence of the President.
- The Vice President shall be elevated to the office of President for the **unexpired term should the president's office becomes vacant**
- The Vice President shall become acting president upon determination that the president becomes too ill to serve; 2/3 majority vote of the Youth Association is required.

Vacancies – The office of Vice President shall be filled by a special election should it become vacant, except that no special election is held less than 30 days prior to the close of the year.

Section D - Secretary

The qualifications of the Secretary shall be a member of the Association; a trustworthy and a patient person; and shall be elected at the same time as the President.

Vacancies – The office of Secretary shall be filled with a special election should it become vacant, except that no special election shall be held less than sixty days prior to the close of the year. The Youth Association will appoint an acting secretary to serve until the new secretary is elected.

Section E – Treasurer

The qualifications of the Treasurer shall be the same as those specified for the secretary.

Authority and duties:

- The treasurer of the association shall serve as the bookkeeper for all monies associated with the Youth Association.
- The treasurer shall serve as the temporary secretary and the secretary shall serve as a temporary treasurer when one or the other is absent.

A vacancy in this office shall be filled in the same manner as a vacancy in the office of secretary

Time of Meeting:

The Youth Association shall meet weekly 6:00 to 8:00 p.m. each third day in the week.

Article VIII - Pledge

Before entering upon their duties, all officers of the Youth Association of the Mt. Calvary Church (or any subdivision) shall make the following pledge in the presence of the president of the association. "I hereby pledge to every citizen of this church community to use all my powers to strengthen and uphold the ideas of the Youth Association of Mt. Calvary Church, which are individual responsibility, loyalty and honor." The new officers of the Youth Association of Mt. Calvary Church shall make this pledge in the presence of the returning officers and youth body.

Article IX - Ratification

This constitution shall take effect immediately upon ratification by 2/3 majority of the Youth Association.

Council Regulation: By Laws

1. Playing and rude behavior will not be tolerated during the time of official business.
2. Each member should conduct themselves in a Christian manner.
3. Members will be recognized during business meetings by raising their hand.
4. Members shall not in any way interfere with the comfort or rights of others.
5. Each member will be given an equal chance to express him or herself in a proper manner.
6. There will be no specific dress code, but each member will be expected to dress appropriately. (The Executive Body have the power to suggests certain types of dress for special occasions.)
7. The Executive Body should conduct themselves accordingly and act only in the best interests of the group as a whole.
8. Any member who persistently acts in an unauthorized manner shall be brought to the attention of the Executive Ministry and questioned as to why they behave in such a manner.
9. Silence all electronics devices cell phones during meetings unless otherwise instructed to use them during an activities

Church Ministry Overview

All believers should be involved in Christian Ministry

According to the Apostle Paul all believers have a spiritual gift but no one possess all of the gifts. Some possess the gift of wisdom others possess the gift of knowledge. The Holy Spirit is the source of all of the spiritual gifts. The Body of Christ is composed of believers who possess different spiritual gifts.

I Corinthians 12: 4,5,6, 8, 20 (KJV)

> 4 Now there are diversities of gifts, but the same Spirit.
> 5 And there are differences of administrations, but the same Lord.
> 6 And there are diversities of operations, but it is the same God which worketh all in all.
> 8 For to one is given by the Spirit the word of wisdom; to another the word of knowledge by the same Spirit;
> 20 But now *are they* many members, yet but one body.

Christian Ministries

(The deacon, trustee, music, stewardship, and the usher **ministries** are listed in other sections of this manual)

Evangelism Ministry

Evangelism is preaching, teaching, witnessing and sharing the good news of Jesus Christ to unsaved men, women, boys and girls. Sharing the good news of Jesus Christ is the primary mission of the church but there are numerous supplementary church missions or ministries.

Jesus says in Matthew 28: 19 "Go ye therefore, and teach all nations, baptizing them in the name of the Father, and of the Son, and of the Holy Ghost:"

All believers are called to share the good news of the Jesus Christ. Evangelism is not just the responsibility of the pastor, Sunday school teachers, deacons, or trustees. The entire Church membership is responsible for evangelizing.

Philippians 2: 10-12 says " That at the name of Jesus every knee should bow, of *things* in heaven, and *things* in earth, and *things* under the earth; **11**And *that* every tongue should confess that Jesus Christ *is* Lord, to the glory of God the Father. All believers have a job to perform in the Kingdom of God.

Evangelism Objective

- Pray for the salvation of the unsaved
- Share the good news of Jesus Christ
- Nurture and provide training for new believers until they are able to lead others to Christ
- Promote an evangelistic outreach program
- Teach the unsaved about the blessings of heaven and the penalty of hell

Church Education Ministry

Another mission of the church is to promote or institute a strong Christian education program. Training believers to be effective ambassadors for Jesus Christ is essential for the programming and the development of effective Christian missions. Christian education programs are needed to help develop strong Christian character which is needed today.

Christian Education Objectives

- Sponsor Christian education seminars and workshops
- Provide a platform for current event discussions that impact Christian life
- Inform the church leadership of essential Christian education needs
- Highlight the importance of essential Christian education material, financial, building and spiritual resources
- Promote Christian education goals and objectives

Elderly Ministry

Ministry to the elderly and the less fortunate is an essential church mission. The bible says honor your mother and your father so that your days will be long on earth. The bible does not specifically mention ministering to the elderly but it stresses the importance of respecting the dignity of the elderly when it says honor your mother and father so that your days will long on earth.

Elderly Objectives

- Teach the importance of respecting the dignity of the elderly
- Encourage senior citizen communication and visitation
- Sponsor senior social programs
- Sponsor spiritual growth programs
- Sponsor senior benefits workshops and seminars
- Sponsor senior outings

Sick and shut-in, less fortunate Ministry

We need to follow the example of Jesus in ministering to the sick. Jesus showed love and compassion to a woman who had an issue of blood for 12 long years, he gave sight to the blind, food to the hungry and he opened the ears of the deaf and allowed the lame to walk. Christians should visit the sick and shut-in, rest homes and hospitals, it is important to show love and compassion for the sick and the less fortunate.

Objectives

- Have an organized sick and shut-in ministry team
- Pray for the healing and restoration of the sick
- Encourage all church members to visit the sick and shut-in
- Have a sick assistance fund
- Provide worship service videos and tapes

Prison Ministry

The church is in the business of ministering to the needs of people regardless of their condition or circumstance. Forgiving and reforming broken lives is an essential Christian ministry. Ministering to prisoners is one of the noblest Christian ministries; showing unconditional love speaks to the very core of the Christian faith.

Objectives

- Have an organized prison visitation ministry
- Provide bibles and other small gifts
- Write letters of encouragement
- Share words of hope and encouragement
- Let prisoners know that they are loved
- Assist prisoners to readjust public life
- Form a prisoner support group
- If possible preach and teach the word to prisoners

Family Development Ministry

Family development is an essential Church ministry or mission. The entertainment media complex has produced programs which are not youth and family friendly. The church must sponsor programs to lead non-believers to Christ and encourage fellow believers to live a Christian lifestyle by avoiding cheating, lying, cussing, drinking, smoking, sex outside of marriage and adultery.

Objective

- Sponsor positive relationship seminars and workshops
- Provide social outlet opportunities
- Find ways to counter the negative influence of the entertainment media complex
- Sponsor marriage enrichment retreats
- Offer parenting classes
- Sponsor social group outings

Men's Ministry

Men have a grave responsibility, according to Psalms 8:4 Man was made a little lower than the angels; he had dominion over the Garden of Eden and everything that lived in the garden. Men will have to give an account of their stewardship. It is time for men to get serious about their Christian stewardship. Men must love their wives and be strong role models for their children and other young people.

Objectives

- Sponsor workshops and seminars that deal with the spiritual growth and development of men
- Serve as role models for young boys
- Have scheduled men bible studies
- Encourage men to pray and read the scripture
- Make men aware of their responsibilities
- Develop programs that keep men engaged in ministry
- Encourage men to use their spiritual gifts
- Encourage the men to develop their own spiritual projects
- Emphasize the importance of proper diet and exercise
- Encourage men to take care of their emotional and physical health

Women's Ministry

Woman was taken from the rib of man close to his heart. Women have a maternal nature that equips them to minister to their husbands and children in a unique way. Over the years women have joined the church in groves. In many ways women are the backbone of the church. Women have a grave responsibility to set a positive example in their dress, speech and behavior. During the early years women tend to influence children more than men therefore; women need to be aware of their unique accountability in God's Kingdom.

Objectives

- Mentor youth and young adult women
- Develop programs to assist children

- Sponsor workshops and seminars on Women's spiritual wellbeing, physical health and other issues
- Invite outside groups to talk on spiritual subjects
- Work with the pastor on special projects
- Have regular bible and prayer sessions
- Share outside workshop information

Youth Ministry (additional Young Ministry information is found in other sections of this manual)

Youth self-esteem programs are also an essential Church mission. The church must support parents in teaching children and youth to respect authority. Youth also must be taught about their heritage, black history programs are essential because history writers do not always highlight the contributions of black American singers', politicians, artists, scientists and inventors. We must teach youth about their history and their heritage.

Objectives

- Have an organized prayer and bible study program
- Provide sufficient recreational opportunities
- Teach about heritage and culture
- Teach youth about money and fiscal management
- Encourage youth to respect authority
- Teach sex education
- Expose youth to positive role models
- Sponsor group outings
- Involve youth in the worship and music ministry
- Provide academic and tutoring assistance
- Sponsor specific youth oriented programs such as fashion and talent shows, drama productions etc.
- Talk about the importance of personal responsibility
- Encourage youth to use appropriate language
- Stress the importance of appropriate dress
- Encourage youth to be on guard against sexual predators and abusive behavior
- Teach youth about dating and positive relationships
- Promote music involvement such as praise teams, choirs etc.

Sunday School, Church Training, Bible Study and Prayer ministries

Christian training and prayer programs are essential for the spiritual development of Church members. All Church ministries should address the unique needs of diverse age groups such as children, youth, young adults, adults and seniors and they also need to address the unique spiritual needs of married couples and singles. The Church is accountable for effective Christian missions and programs.

Church ministries must address individual age group. Each age has its own unique needs. Age appropriate programs are essential for the growth and the spiritual development of believers.

Sunday school (additional Sunday school is listed in another section of this manual)

Sunday school is not just for children; all church members should attend Sunday school. The blue print of living a Christian life is embedded in the School curriculum. .

The Importance of Church Training (additional Church Training is important and is found in other sections of this manual)

Church Training is essential for teaching standard Christian doctrine, Church policy and procedure.

Objectives

- Expose members to a variety of teaching methods
- Emphasize the importance of prayer and bible study
- Have scheduled weekly ongoing training programs
- Stress the importance of being consistent and devoted to all spiritual tasks
- Promote spiritual growth and development
- Highlight the importance of patience and devotion

Prayer Ministry

James 5:16 says:

> [16] Confess *your* trespasses[a] to one another, and pray for one another, that you may be healed. The effective, fervent prayer of a righteous man avails much. King James Version (NKJV)

Prayer is essential in a Christians life. Each should have a strong pray ministry

Objectives

- Encourage members to pray on a continuous basis
- Have a regular meeting the same time each week
- Encourage private and group prayers
- Allow participants to call out the name of people or events or occurrences to be prayed for
- Pray before making a major decision which will affect the life of the church
- Pray for the church leadership and membership
- Discuss the importance of prayer
- Sponsor prayer workshops and seminars

Hospitality or Hosting Ministry

A friendly smile and a kind word can go a long way in attracting new members. People want to feel loved and appreciated. The hospitality committee should be staffed by Church members who are friendly in nature and have the people skills to assist in the growth and development of the church.

Those who serve on the hospitality committee are usually the first church greeters. First impressions are extremely important. There is no way to undo a first impression. There is a saying "First impressions are golden" this is extremely true in a church setting.

Objective

- Greet others with kind words and a friendly loving smile
- Dispense church literature and handouts

- Greet incoming and outing members and visitors
- Answer visitor questions
- Project a sense of confidence, faith and love
- Assist ushers when called on
- Assist with food and special program events

Recreation Ministry

Fun and recreation is a part of church life. Jesus attended weddings and he ministered to large gathering such as the time he feed 5,000 people. Most of his ministerial work was outdoors in open areas; common men, women, boys and girls were the central focus of Jesus ministries.

Objectives

- Involve youth and members in team oriented sports such as basketball, softball, soccer etc.
- Sponsor exercise or walking programs
- Supervise youth recreational activities
- Educate members on the importance of exercise and recreation

Outreach Ministry

Each church should have an effective outreach ministry. The true church extends beyond the walls of a wood or brick structure. It is all about ministering to others who live in the community. There are a lot of hurting people who do not attend church; they need to be ministered to. The Church outreach ministry also aids in church membership growth and development.

Objectives

- Highlight the importance of evangelism and salvation
- Aid the pastor in attracting new members
- Develop strategies to minister to those who do not attend church
- Dispense evangelist and church invitation literature
- Use the print media, audio media, phone calls, emails, face book, twitter and other social media to invite and promote church attendance, extraordinary events and other programs

New members/support ministry

New members need to be enrolled in a new member's class. The class should highlight the scriptural teaching of tithing, a review of the church's Covenant, Constitution and Bylaws along with standard Church Doctrine.

It is up to the church to customize a personal new member's class. It could be 10 or more hours of instructions. Upon completing a new members class; members should be encouraged to serve in one or more church ministries, it could be the music, the usher or the recreational ministry. The pastor has the option of subjecting were new members should serve.

Support team ministry

A support team should be made up of spiritually mature Christians. A husband and wife team would be ideal. The team will provide support for incoming members throughout their spiritual journey. Incoming members are encouraged to call their support team if they desire prayer, or if they have questions or a problem within the church.

Objectives

- Pray for the spiritual growth of new members
- Sponsor new members orientation classes
- Highlight church doctrine explain church policy
- Help new members transition into church ministries
- Mentor, counsel, support incoming members
- Work with the pastor to acquire an appropriate new member's curriculum

Media/ News Letter/ Technology Ministry

A positive current news ministry is needed in the church. A church newsletter can be a tremendous ministry promotional and educational tool. The church community needs to share positive uplifting news.

Technology Ministry

The world is continuously changing. The information age has taken root. It is essential that church take advantage of new emerging technologies. LCD projectors, computers and large screen monitors are a few of the technologies that have made a difference in dispensing information in many of our progressive churches. Young people live in a world of face book, twitter and many other social networks. It is time to use technologies to dispense essential spiritual wisdom and knowledge.

Objectives

- Publish religious, health, family, cultural heritage and other appropriate information
- Promote events and programs
- Find ways to use technology to air spiritual programs
- Use technology to save and better manage time
- Provide opportunities for young people to use technology

Landscape/ Car Parking/ Beautification Ministry

- Beautify outdoor church grounds
- Help to keep the inside of the church cleaned and sanitized
- Aid in cutting grass, planting flowers
- Supervise the cleaning of the church's gravesite
- Suggest future beautification projects
- Assist in parking cars and other physical church projects

Now that we have defined Christian missions and Christian ministries; the question is "How can we effectively promote Church sponsored ministries and programs?"

- First of all church workers must be born again; the blind cannot lead the blind.
- All believers must pray for the guidance of the Holy Spirit. 1John 4:4: **says** "Ye are of God, little children, and have overcome them: because greater is he that is in you, than he that is in the world"

183

Believers can choose to walk in the spirit or walk in the flesh. Those who walk in the spirit will not fulfill the lust of the flesh. Walking in the spirit means possessing the Fruit of the Spirit. The Fruit of the Spirit are listed in Galatians 5: "22 But the Fruit of the Spirit is love, joy, peace, longsuffering, gentleness, goodness, faith, 23Meekness, temperance: against such there is no law."

When others see the Fruit of the Spirit in a Christian workers life; effective promotion of Christian missions is enhanced. http://bible.cc/galatians/5-18.htmWe must also be aware that accountability for effective Christian missions can only be achieved through the power and the unifying force of the Holy Spirit.

- Those who effectively promote Christian missions and Christian programs must be united as one in the Spirit; believers must work together for the goal of winning others to Christ.

- To achieve the goal of unity and harmony we must look at the relationship that Jesus had with his heavenly father. The Father and Jesus were of the same Mind and the same Spirit there was no division between the Heavenly Father and Jesus. We must be united if we are to achieve the goals and the objectives of the church. Unity in the Spirit is one of the major keys to accountability for effective Christian Missions.

- Those who possess various Spiritual Gifts must work together. If there is a division in the church the accountability for effective Christian missions will not be achieved. It is essential for believers who have different gifts and talents to work together for a common cause. Those who have the Gift of teaching must work with those who have the Gift of knowledge and Wisdom. The world must see the love of Jesus in a believers personal lives, Believers must send positive Christian signals to those who live in the world, we must send the signals of the Fruit of the Spirit: love, peace joy, patience and longsuffering.

Other essential factors to achieve accountability for effective Christian missions

- Churches are encouraged to have specific time slots for Church training and Christian education programs. It could be one or two Sunday evening time slots. Dates and time slots can be adjusted to address the needs of the church.

- Each Church has a personality. Christian education workers should work with the pastor to assign a specific time slot for Christian education training.

- Church leaders should do everything in their power to make sure that they are taking advantage of positive Christian resources that are available to help their church to promote and achieve effective Christian missions.

- The Word of God which is the Holy Scripture holds the key to promoting effective Christian missions. Each person is encouraged to read and study the Word of God and pray for understanding to address the accountability for effective Christian missions.

NOTES

1. Christian Education Model

All scripture references were taken from the "King James Bible"(Camden: Thomas Nelson Inc. 1972)

1 Carlisle Driggers, Ridgecrest Baptist Conference Center lecture, August 1982, information on Planning.

2 Ibid.

3 Ibid.

Kenneth D. Blazier, Evelyn M. Huber, Planning Christian Education in Your Church (Valley Forge: Judson Press, 1974) was a very good resource book giving ideas on planning and writing goals and objectives.

2. Church Personnel Job Descriptions & Qualifications

Kenneth D. Blazier, Teaching Church at Work (Valley Forge: Judson Press 1980) was a very good source in writing on Church Personnel Job Descriptions & Qualifications.

3. Resources

Kenneth D. Blazier, Evelyn M. Huber, Planning Christian Education in Your Church (Valley Forge: Judson Press, 1974) was a very good resource book giving great ideas on church resources.

4. Importance of Time Management

Speed B. Leas, Time Management - A Working Guide for Leaders (Nashville: Parthenon Press 1978) was a very good source in writing on time management.

5. The Psychology of Age Groups

1 Harry M. Piland, Basic School Work (Nashville: Convention Press 1980) p. 158.

2 Ibid., p. 158.

3 Ibid., p. 159.

Kenneth D. Blazier, Evelyn M. Huber, Planning Christian Education in Your Church (Valley
Forge: Judson Press 1974) was a very good resource on age groups.

6. Ushering

All scripture references were taken from the King James Bible (Camden: Thomas Nelson Inc.
1971).

1 Noah Webster LL.D, Webster's Dictionary (New York: Modern Publishing 1984) p. 348.

Thomas L. Clark, A Guide for the Church Usher (Nashville: Broadman Press 1984) was a very
good source.

7. Sunday School

The Sunday School section is written from the author's personal observation of Sunday School
work expanding over a thirty year period.

8. Church Training

1 J. M. Caldwell, Baptist Training Union and Christian Education Workbook (Evansville: Aztec
Printing, Inc. 1984) p. 32.

2 Ibid. p. 32.

3 Ibid. p. 33.

4 Ibid. p. 20.

All scripture references were taken from the King James Bible (Camden: Thomas Nelson Inc.
1972).

9. Qualities of Christian Leaders

The leadership section is written from the author's personal observations of Christian qualities observed over a thirty year period.

All scripture references were taken from the King James Bible (Camden: Thomas Nelson Inc. 1972).

10. Traditional Christian Beliefs

All scripture references were taken from the King James Bible (Camden: Thomas Nelson Inc. 1972).

W.E. Vine, Merrill F Unger, William White, Jr. The Hiscox Vines Complete Expository Dictionary 1 (Nashville: Thomas Nelson Publishers

11. How to Remain Christian in an Un-Christian Environment

Scripture references were checked against passages in the King James Bible (Camden: Thomas Nelson Inc. 1972).

12. The Church

Scripture references were checked against passages in the King James Bible (Camden: Thomas Nelson Inc. 1972).

1 William C. Martin, The Layman's Bible Encyclopedia (Nashville: The Southwestern Company, 1964) p. 147.

13. Church Music

1 William C. Martin, The Layman's Bible Encyclopedia (Nashville: The Southwestern Company, 1964) p. 547.

2 Walter Hines Sims, Baptist Hymnal (Nashville: Convention Press, 1956) p. 535-537.

3 Bernard S. Cayne, The New Lexicon, Webster's Dictionary (New York: Lexicon Publications, Inc. 1989) p. 38.

4 Ibid. p. 958.

5 Emmanuel L. McCall, The Black Christian Experience (Nashville: Broadman Press, 1972) p. 69.

6 Martin, p. 292

14. Stewardship and Tithing

1 Bennett W. Smith, Handbook on Tithing (Elgin: Progressive Baptist Publishing House) p. 25.

2 Ibid. p. 25.

All scripture references were taken from the King James Bible
    Camden: Thomas Nelson Inc., 1972)

15. Deacons

1 William C. Martin, The Layman's Bible Encyclopedia (Nashville: The Southwestern Company, 1964) p. 187.

2 Edward T. Hiscox, The Hiscox Standard Baptist Manual (Valley Forge: The Judson Press, 1981) p. 57.

All scripture references were taken from the King James Bible(Camden: Thomas Nelson Inc., 1972).

16. Trustees

1 Edward T. Hiscox, The Hiscox Standard Baptist Manual (Valley Forge: The Judson Press, 1981) p. 72.

2 Glenn H. Asquith, Church Officers at Work (Valley Forge: The Judson Press, 1951) p. 54.

17. Sample Youth Program

The position and duty section of this paper was fashioned after a 1980 Organizing A Baptist Student Union bulletin by: National Student Ministries, Nashville, Tennessee.

The section on maintaining a good youth program was fashioned after a 1980 Organizing A Baptist Student Union on a Predominantly Black College Campus by National Student Ministries in Nashville, Tennessee.

18. Sample Youth Worship Service

All scripture references were taken from the King James Bible (Camden: Thomas Nelson Inc., 1972).

The author wrote the sermon entitled "Ambition" portraying the tragedy of William Shakespeare's Macbeth in 1984 when he was a seminary student. (Resource: Knickerbocker, K. L.; Reninger, Willard H. book, Interpreting Literature)

19. Sample Church and Youth Constitution

The author served as volunteer Youth Director for the Mount Calvary Baptist Church in 1970 where he edited and wrote the final draft of the Youth Constitution listed in the Sample Youth Constitution section of this handbook

Bibliography

Aldridge, Marion D., The Pastor's Guidebook - A Manual for Worship.
    Nashville: Broadman Press, 1984.

Asquith, Glenn H., Church Officers at Work. Valley Forge: The Judson Press, 1951.

Blazier, Kenneth D., The Teaching Church at Work. Valley Forge: The Judson Press, 1980.

Caldwell, J. M., Baptist Training Union and Christian Education Workbook.
    Evansville: Aztec Printing, Inc., 1984.

Carrier, Wallace H., Teaching Adults in Sunday School. Nashville: Convention Press, 1976.

Cayne, Bernard S., The New Lexicon, Webster's Dictionary.
    New York: Lexicon Publications, Inc., 1989.

Church Training Staff, Equipping and Developing Believers. Raleigh:
    Baptist State Convention Press, 1984.

Clark, Thomas L., A Guide for the Church Usher. Nashville: Broadman Press, 1984.

Dowley, Tim, Eerdmans' Handbook to the History of Christianity.
    Grand Rapids: Wm. B. Eerdmans' Publishing Co., 1977.

Driggers, Carlisle, Ridgecrest: Baptist Conference Center,
    Lecture Information on Planning, 1982.

Foshee, Howard B., The Church Usher. Nashville: Convention Press.

Hobbs, Herschel H., The Baptist Faith and Message. Nashville: Convention Press, 1971.

Hiscox, Edward T., The Hiscox Standard Baptist Manual. Valley Forge: The Judson Press, 1981.

Knickerbocker, K. L.; Reninger, Willard H., Interpreting Literature.
    New York: Holt Rinehart and Winston, 1965.

Leas, Speed B., Time Management - A Working Guide for Leaders. Nashville: Parthenon Press, 1978.

Martin, Williams C., The Layman's Bible Encyclopedia. Nashville: The Southwestern Company, 1964.

McCall, Emmanuel L., The Black Christian Experience. Nashville: Broadman Press, 1972.

Piland, Harry M., Basic Sunday School Work. Nashville: Convention Press, 1980.

Powers, Bruce P., Christian Education Handbook. Nashville: Convention Press, 1981.

Scripture References, King James Bible. Camden: Thomas Nelson, Inc., 1972.

Sims, Walter Hines, Baptist Hymnal. Nashville: Convention Press, 1956.

Smith, Bennett W., Handbook on Tithing. Elgin: Progressive Baptist Publishing House.

Strickland, Jenell, How to Guide Preschoolers. Nashville: Convention *Press, 1982.*

Terrell, Jerry, Basic Preschool Work. Nashville: Convention Press, 1981.

Webster, Noah LL.D., Webster's Dictionary. New York: Modern Publishing, 1984.

Young, William E., "The Church Ushering Committee" Nashville:

The Sunday School Board of the Southern Baptist Convention, 1977

Printed in the United States
By Bookmasters